DATE DUE			

PERGAMON INTERNATIONAL LIBRARY
of Science, Technology, Engineering and Social Studies

The 1000-volume original paperback library in aid of education,
industrial training and the enjoyment of leisure

Publisher: Robert Maxwell, M.C.

The Social Cost of Small Families and Land Reform

A Case Study of the Wataita of Kenya

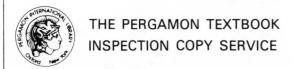

International Population Series, Volume 1
EPSTEIN & JACKSON
The Feasibility of Fertility Planning

Other Titles of Interest
ABDULLAH and ZEIDENSTEIN
Village Women of Bangladesh: Prospects for Change

EPSTEIN and WATTS
The Endless Day: Some Case Material on Asian Rural Women

GULATI
Profiles in Female Poverty: A Study of Five Poor Working Women in Kerala

NELSON
Why has Development Neglected Rural Women?

SEARLE-CHATTERJEE
Reversible Sex-Roles: The Special Case of Benares Sweepers

Related Journal
WORLD DEVELOPMENT*
The multidisciplinary journal devoted to the study and promotion of world
development

Chairman of the Editorial Board:
Dr Paul Streeten, Center for Asian Development Studies, Boston University,
264 Bay State Rd., Boston, MA 02215, USA

*Free specimen copy available on request

The Social Cost of Small Families and Land Reform

A Case Study of the Wataita of Kenya

by

GEORGE C. MKANGI
University of Nairobi, Kenya

with special assistance from Gwen Jones

With a foreword by

DAVID PARKIN
University of London

PERGAMON PRESS
OXFORD · NEW YORK · TORONTO · SYDNEY · PARIS · FRANKFURT

U.K.	Pergamon Press Ltd., Headington Hill Hall, Oxford OX3 0BW, England
U.S.A.	Pergamon Press Inc., Maxwell House, Fairview Park, Elmsford, New York 10523, U.S.A.
CANADA	Pergamon Press Canada Ltd., Suite 104, 150 Consumers Rd., Willowdale, Ontario M2J 1P9, Canada
AUSTRALIA	Pergamon Press (Aust.) Pty. Ltd., P.O. Box 544, Potts Point, N.S.W. 2011, Australia
FRANCE	Pergamon Press SARL, 24 rue des Ecoles, 75240 Paris, Cedex 05, France
FEDERAL REPUBLIC OF GERMANY	Pergamon Press GmbH, Hammerweg 6, D-6242 Kronberg-Taunus, Federal Republic of Germany

Copyright ©1983 George C. Mkangi

First edition 1983

Library of Congress Cataloging in Publication Data
Mkangi. George C.
The social cost of small families and land reform.
(International population series; 2)
1. Taita (African people)—Economic conditions.
2. Taita (African people)—Social conditions.
3. Land tenure—Kenya. 4. Kenya—Population policy.
5. Birth control—Kenya. 6. Family size—Kenya.
7. Kenya—Economic conditions—1963- . 8. Kenya—
Social conditions. I. Jones, Gwen. II. Title.
III. Series.
DT433.545.T34M58   1983   330.9676'204'089963   82-16618

British Library Cataloguing in Publication Data
Mkangi, George C.
The social cost of small families and land
reform.—(International population series; 2)
1. Taita (Bantu tribe)—Population
2. Land reform—Kenya
I. Title   II. Series
304.6'2'096762   DT433.542
ISBN 0-08-028952-5

In order to make this volume available as economically and as rapidly as possible the authors' typescripts have been reproduced in their original forms. This method unfortunately has its typographical limitations but it is hoped that they in no way distract the reader.

Printed and bound in Great Britain by
William Clowes Limited, Beccles and London

To Scarlett

for adopting and having confidence in me

Foreword

We have recently been made familiar with the distinction between economic
growth and development. The former is assessed by the level of GNP and by
no means necessarily entails the development of equal social opportunities
and a humane society. Because the latter can only be measured by subjective
criteria, it is no less important. Indeed, one would expect it to be
primary. Yet, even nowadays, international aid agencies frequently emphasize
economic expansion as a precondition of, and sometimes as equivalent to,
development in Third World countries. Dr. Mkangi's book is a caustic
reminder of the error of such thinking. He pulls no punches. We recognize
the caricature of the international aid expatriate gathering his findings
from the confines and luxury of the capital city. We are forced to acknowledge some of the inadequacies of a Western life-style that often leads us
to value nuclear family privacy over care for the aged, pets over children,
or children's play with dolls as a substitute for interaction with people.

In particular, the book sets out to show how development policies based on a
Western model do not achieve what is necessarily in the interests of the
mass of rural folk. Dr. Mkangi's data are taken from a small number of
rural households in Taita district, Kenya, in which he lived on a number of
occasions for over a year. He questions the assumption that land reform and
family planning will reduce poverty. On the contrary, he argues, the drive
to adjudicate, register, consolidate, and enclose land, has created strong
barriers between family households whose networks of relations were
traditionally able to absorb and disperse inequalities of wealth and
production. The resultant enduring inequalities in land holding and
production have benefited only a few, while the majority hopelessly seek
security in wage jobs and education for their children.

For this majority, the more children the better. At least one son or
daughter, it is supposed, will one day be able to subsidize the rest of the
family. It is an illusion, and more children become more mouths to feed out
of a diminishing budget. But, says Dr. Mkangi, under the changed conditions
how can we expect people to think otherwise? He recognizes full well that
the rate of population growth in Kenya is colossal. He also notes that Taita
women themselves would welcome family planning under circumstances in which
their families could be guaranteed a secure living standard and meaningful
existence. Dr. Mkangi's recipe is disarmingly simple but dramatic in its

implications: stop or reverse land reform and eliminate the emerging
inequalities, steer peasant production more in the direction of at least
partial self-sufficiency, and, then and only then, we should be able to see
the 'problem' of population growth in its proper perspective.

The argument is convincing. We may also learn from the method. The micro-
sociological study of a small culturally distinct group of ordinary people
should surely precede, not follow, analysis of statistics lodged in city
capitals. For how else shall we discover what the people themselves really
think about the policies made for them by others? How else will such people
as the Taita be able to say which parts of their rich culture, well
documented elsewhere (e.g. G. Harris, 1978), should be preserved?
Dr. Mkangi's book is therefore one of a growing number of intensive investi-
gations in the field of so-called development studies that challenge
entrenched thought and practice.

University of London   DAVID PARKIN

Acknowledgements

It is without doubt that but for Professor T. Scarlett Epstein, this study would not have been carried out at all. For it was she, who as Professorial Fellow at the Institute of Development Studies (IDS), University of Sussex, conceived, did the ground-work and then directed the Project entitled *A Cross-cultural Study of Population Growth and Rural Poverty*. It was a four-year Project running from October 1973 to the autumn of 1977, involving eight students including myself, who conducted field research in India, Kenya, Nigeria and Sri Lanka. Throughout this period, Professor Epstein has been my academic supervisor and guru. She has also been the means of my financial sustenance and, with her maternal caring, a major influence on my social - and in some cases, moral - health. I owe much to her and the completion of this study symbolizes my greatest gratitude.

The funds which enabled me to finish this manuscript and obtain my doctorate from the University of Sussex were contributed by the Population Council and the World Bank. I wish to express my sincere gratitude for this help and hope that this book will provide justification for their support.

It must have been stated many times before, but repeating it will not turn the feelings into a cliché: for the fact is that successful completion of an exercise of this kind is not one man's lone endeavour. Hence I feel bound to acknowledge the comradely support, advice and criticism I received from the other members of the Project, namely: Monica Das Gupta, Mukul Dube, Newton Gunasinghe, Vinod Jairath, Sammy N. Onwuazor, Joseph Ssennyonga and W. M. Tilakaratne. In addition I should mention Darrell Jackson, Tim Dyson, Rosemary Watts, Mariette Grange and Pam Smith.

In Taita where I did my fieldwork, I received every encouragement and help from the Taita/Taveta District Administration, starting with the District Commissioner, Mr. King'uru, and going right through the Administration. Worthy of mention are Chief Kubo of Werugha Location and Sub-Chiefs Moses Washo of Shigaro/Sungululu Sub-location and Samuel Mnjama Kiongo of Werugha Sub-location. In addition I cannot forget my host Noel Mwazera and his family; George Ndegwa, my brother-in-law, who was then the District Magistrate; Mr. Geoffrey Mjomba, Clerk to the County Council; Mgosi Jamiel; the late Rev. Jeremiah Kiwinda and the heads of the sixteen households with whom I worked very closely. These are Samuel Mnjama, Moses Mugho, Failstone

Kinyavura, Jonathan Kiongo, Mama Mary G. Mwamdondo, Augustine N. Shako, Mama
Charlotte Fridah M. Mwakio, Mama Jaridine Mlolwa, Benstone Dishon Kalaghe,
Kirigha Ngali, Mzee Ngali, Mama Sophy Mwangemi, Godiffrey Mwanyama and Noel
Mwazera. Also I should mention my helpers Basil Mwakulegwa, Mary Mwanyumba,
Mary Mjomba and Miss Mwangemi from Shigaro. Teachers and pupils from the
following schools gave me invaluable assistance: Shigaro, Sungululu, Werugha,
Mwakishimba, Ngulu-Kiweto and Mdondonyi Primary Schools and Aggrey and
Mwangeka High Schools.

I have to mention the special and understanding help from Mary Kidelo Righa
and the stimulating and fruitful company of Lydia Mrunde Kubo. In addition
to sharing Wambugha-Chizi, the latter gave me some useful insights into
traditional Taita society.

As for the 'numberless peasants', my greatest regret is that I am unable to
express my gratitude to them in a manner and language that they can both
appreciate and understand. Nevertheless, if through a study like this the
powers-that-be are forced to take a serious hard look at the peasants'
plight, then I will have gone a little way in repaying the warm hospitality
they showed me and the help they gave throughout my stay with them - for
they would rather be recognized than studied.

I am also thankful to the authorities of the Institute of Development Studies
- for the congenial atmosphere they allowed me to work in, especially after
the Population Project officially came to an end in September 1977. My
thanks too to Professors Zev Barbu and Ron Dore for the academic support they
have in one way or another given to me throughout my long stay at the
University of Sussex.

My thanks go to all my friends and relatives who at one time or another
wished me well. Finally and most importantly, my heartfelt gratitude to
Gwen and my family in having confidence in me, showing their patience and
affection throughout my long endeavour to learn the 'White man's book'. As
for Gwen, this work is just as much hers as mine.

To all of you I offer my gratitude and acknowledge your help. As for any
mistakes and shortcomings, they are mine and therefore my responsibility.

Contents

Contents

List of Charts

List of Diagrams

Contents

Introduction

At the outset I think I should declare my approach to the topic in question. Since I myself come from one of the so-called *developing* or *less developed* or *Third World countries*,[1] I do not regard the study of *development* as a mere academic pursuit but as a matter of life and death. As far as I am concerned, poverty is central to the whole theme of development and, as such, exists in reality and not just as a concept. Unfortunately, some of our experts do not regard poverty in this way, as the following 'factitious'[2] story tries to illustrate:

> There was once a consultant expert who went to look at the problems of one of the poorest countries in the world. He went as part of a 'technical aid' programme given by his own country. Since in the long run the poor country had to pay back the 'aid' given, plus interest, to the rich 'donor' country, it is not difficult to see that the real employer of our expert was in fact the poor country.
>
> Taking a stroll around the dusty city centre (in real life such experts do not walk - unless looking for curios or exploring beauty spots or national parks - but are driven around), our expert was several times confronted by beggars who kept thrusting their boney, dirty hands at him, begging.
>
> At the end of his consultancy he produced a 'Plan' (which he had drawn up before coming to the country), but now with one important addition. He wrote "The beggars are an eye-sore and the Government is well advised to pass legislation forbidding begging in the city centres if it desires to attract tourists to this beautiful country. . . ."

---

[1] These countries make up two-thirds of the world's population (Sauvy, 1975: 97).

[2] The word comes from faction, which is a derivative of both *fact* and *fiction*. Faction has a true factual base, though apparently imagined.

On this score, Myrdal (1971: 17) has this to say: "Place the economist in
the capital of an underdeveloped country and give him the necessary assistance and he will in no time make a Plan." The point of this story is to
show how and to what extent poverty has been conceptualized and that its
real existence is no longer recognized even when one comes face to face with
it.[3] Such a conceptualization enables one to regard poverty as yet another
problem for 'developing' countries to tackle rather than as the core problem
endemic to a 'developing' country.

In order to understand what the term development means and before attempting
to define it, one has to be conscious of a historical process whereby wealth
- whether in the form of land, cattle or money - first attained life of its
own. This happened when wealth underwent a metamorphosis through which it
encapsulated within itself an immense dynamism which had both the ability to
generate and the potential to sustain limitless economic development. This
dynamism is inherent in the circulation of wealth in the form of money,
since every circulation finishes by reactivating yet another circulation.

> Money ends the movement only to begin it again. Therefore, the final
> result of every separate circuit, in which a purchase and consequent
> sale are completed, forms itself the starting-point of a new circuit.
> The simple circulation of commodities - selling in order to buy - is a
> means of carrying out a purpose unconnected with circulation, namely,
> the appropriation of use-values, the satisfaction of wants. *The
> circulation of money as capital is, on the contrary, an end in itself,
> for the expansion of value takes place only within this constantly
> renewed movement. The circulation of capital has therefore no limits.*
> (Karl Marx, *Capital*, Vol. One, Part II, Chapter IV: 150; emphasis
> added.)

Hence wealth in the form of money undergoes a qualitative change and it is
in its qualitatively transformed state that it ceases to be just money and
becomes capital.

Thus development, in the modern sense of the word, is first and foremost
brought about by the existence of capital. But the kind of development
capital can bring about is determined by the dominant social forces within
the total societal environment in which capital emerges. Historically, the
transformation of wealth (in this case, money) into capital first took place
in Western European societies, which in their feudal stage had attained a
high degree of differentiation. The subsequent economic development
triggered off by capital expanded and accelerated and went on to consolidate
the position of the dominant stratum within the stratified societies. In so
doing, the surplus generated by capital was maldistributed in favour of the
dominant stratum. Thus, since capital was bound within a specific and
particularistic socio-cultural milieu, it inevitably transferred its ethos
as it expanded.

For development to become a scientific endeavour, the historical and sociological study of capital *per se* is imperative. The question of capital's
expansion and its ability to create a global system for itself becomes
crucial. In addition, its ability to co-opt, distort or maintain certain

---

[3]The conceptualization is so thorough that debilitating poverty existing in
developed countries - such as in the urban ghettos or rural areas in the
southern states of the U.S.A. - attracts little analytical academic attention
as compared with its counterpart in the less developed countries (ldc's).

social structures, especially when expanding into pre-capitalistic
societies,[4] without losing its primary function - that is, the expropriation
of surplus from these areas - becomes a central issue if one is to understand
development. For at different levels and at different times, capital has
thrust to the fore sociological (in retrospect, historical) phenomena such
as European migration to the Americas, Australia, New Zealand and South
Africa; the slave trade; colonialism; the modern wars; racism; and overt and
covert imperialism. All these phenomena are rooted in capital. Thus the
historical and sociological context within which capital emerges and from
which it operates must be understood because it is within this context that
social, political, economic and academic arguments are produced to deny the
fact that within capital's capacity to develop also lies its capacity to
underdevelop.

What has until recently passed for the study of development in the Third
World has in fact been a documentation of underdevelopment, which is a result
and an integral part of the whole of capital's dynamism. Being a documentation of underdevelopment, the exercise fails to grapple with the scientific
existence of the reality under examination. Hence it is not surprising that
the study of development is associated with a collection of facts and
figures imbued with ethnocentrism. The manifestation of this ethnocentricity
is embodied first and foremost in certain current academic assumptions that
the economic development of the underdeveloped parts of the globe, of the
Third World especially, can be effected without confronting the central
issue that the initial and continuing underdevelopment of the Third World is
the inexorable and concomitant function of capital developing other parts of
the globe - namely, the industrialized world. In other words, development
and underdevelopment are rarely regarded as two sides of a single process.[5]
The result of this academic 'oversight' is the incessant production of
theories which fail to explain the emergence of the phenomenon euphemistically
known as *ldc's* and also the persistence of underdevelopment (typified in the
widening of the gap between the rich and poor of the world) in spite of the
orchestrated attack on the problem since the 1950s.

So far the theories produced have been largely descriptive of the state of
underdeveloped countries. Such theories are consequently replete with
ethnocentrism and thus have no alternative to empiricism to show that they are
'scientific'. The 'modernization' theory is one example. According to this
theory, development is an evolutionary process whereby a society moves from
a 'tribal' stage to a 'modern' stage; from 'simple' to 'complex'; 'rural' to
'urban'; 'particularistic' to 'universalistic'; 'less developed' to
'developed', and so on. Its exponents do not even recognize the existence
of the capital, let alone its potency. All they can do is to offer an
analytical and descriptive framework for comparing societies on a continuum
of 'ideal types'. The terms 'tribal', 'simple', 'rural', 'particularistic'
and 'less developed' approximate to what are known as the Third World
countries; while 'modern', 'complex', 'urban', 'universalistic' and
'developed' approximate to what are known as the industrialized countries of

---

[4]Indeed in some cases capital's expansion has contributed to the total
extermination of a society. I have in mind the extermination of the Caribs
in the Caribbean Islands and the indigenous population of Tasmania (see
Rodney, 1972: 18).

[5]For an understanding of the historic-sociological relationship between
development and underdevelopment, see Baran and Sweezy, 1966; Rodney *op.
cit.*, especially Chapter One. Frank, 1969; Baran, 1957.

the 'Western World'.[6] There is no attempt to grasp the symbiotic relationship between the two polar ends of the continuum.

An extension of the 'modernization' theory is the economic theory of
'dualism', which questions the treatment of the two poles of the continuum
as independent and unconnected entities. In general terms, the 'dual economy'
theory does recognize a sort of connectedness but only a tenuous one, in
which the backward rural sector has nothing to offer the dynamic, modern
urban sector except labour, raw materials and food (Boeke, 1968; R. Meier,
1965; Rostow, 1967). Since the connection is assumed to be tenuous, this
theory does not depart much from 'modernization theory', in that both
minimize the contribution the rural sector makes in the form of labour, raw
materials and food, and overemphasize the role played by the modern urban
sector within the national economy. Thus both theories hold the two poles
of the continuum as essentially independent and unconnected. With this
assumption, it is taken for granted that, for example, the backward rural
sector is self-sufficient in its basic need and what it releases to the
modern urban sector is a surplus which it is happy to part with. Thus the
labour it supplies is that which it does not itself require, and the labour
released is not seen to be people responding to an economic reality, but to
be rather hordes of migrants who, for lack of better things to do in their
rural homes, migrate to the urban areas. Within the modern urban sector
they are regarded as migrants[7] and not as workers and, as migrants, they are
expected to return to their rural homes. In addition, since they are
supposed to come from a self-sufficient rural sector, the 'dual economy'
theory justifies paying depressed wages to these migrant labourers.[8]

Nevertheless, it was the 'dual economy' theory which provided the
modernization approach to development with its economic rationale. That is
why in the 1950s and early 1960s 'development studies' were the domain of
economists and current practice was to define development using economistic
measurement indices such as Gross National Product (GNP) and Gross Domestic
Product (GDP).[9] It was the 'failure' of this economistic approach[10] –
rather than the inherent failure to define development scientifically – which
led to it being regarded as inadequate in explaining the persistence of
poverty as a consequence of underdevelopment in the less developed countries.
But instead of questioning the fundamental issue, which is the persistence
of poverty, the fault was thought to lie in the economistic approach to
development. To rectify this situation it was thought that development
would be better tackled if it were done with an interdisciplinary approach.[11]

---

[6]This includes Japan, Australia, New Zealand and South Africa.

[7]In other situations they are regarded as hordes of the urban unemployed
or underemployed who live by being active in the "Informal Sector" of the
economy!

[8]South Africa is the example *par excellence* where the dual economy theory
has been carried out to its non-scientific and dehumanized limits.

[9]See 'Capital Accumulation' in Meier, 1964.

[10]See Seers, 1972.

[11]See Celso Furtado, "Development", in *International Social Science Journal*,
Vol. XXIX, No. 4, 1977; especially pp.635-649.

In general, the interdisciplinary method sees the failure to eradicate poverty as being due either to the existence of certain 'obstacles', or to the non-existence of certain variables such as McClelland's need for achievement' (1961) or entrepreneurial skills and values such as those propounded by Talcott Parsons (1964). This approach does not define development nor does it see the structural process of development and under-development as an integral whole, with both aspects issuing from the dynamic of capital. On the whole, there is too much emphasis on proving Marxism wrong and not enough on understanding the historic-sociological dynamism of capital and its adaptability.[12] For it is its inexhaustible dynamism and adaptability which makes development generated by capital historic-sociologically determined and hence scientific.

To deny this leaves one with the ethnocentric-orientated bias found in the current approaches to and definitions of development. Thus the non-occurrence of economic development in the *ldc*'s is explained through a cyclical trial-and-error 'hobby horsing' of perceived problems and obstacles.[13] Examples of such 'obstacles' are: lack of skilled manpower, high unemployment, income maldistribution, population growth, communal land tenure and many others; their 'rise and fall' depend very much on how far they catch the fancy of social scientists (and the support of their funding bodies).

But armed with no specific general law or theory to explain why less developed countries remain poor despite all the efforts to develop them, this school of thought hopes to ameliorate the cyclical approach within an interdisciplinary framework by developing rigorous research methodologies for the collection of empirical data on the perceived 'obstacles'. The main objective of these methodologies is not to discover a law which explains how the obstacle came into existence, but frequently becomes the test of the data. The overriding concern is how far the data have been collected scientifically instead of how far the data correspond with reality. Indeed, obsession with the scientific validity of the data becomes an end in itself. In the search for 'empirical reality' there is no room for the realization that the 'obstacle' under investigation is but a manifestation of reality and of the dynamic of capital.

I regard problems of population growth and land distribution as 'obstacles' to economic development only in the sense that they are symptomatic of problems generated by capitalism. Since the country in question (Kenya) is an appendage of this system, the complexities inherent in these obstacles are simply manifestations of the dynamic of capital in generating simultan-eously both development and underdevelopment, especially in the way it was introduced into the country (see Chapter 3).

---

[12]For example, Long, 1977, considers the 'Structural Dependency' thesis too simplistic (p.85); he thus substitutes for it an ethno-reductionist argument of his own (p.89) and finishes up by trivializing it (pp.90-91).

[13]Dudley Seers has gone full cycle when he argues that we should not be talking about *development* any more but about *dependency*. That is, the problem is to see to what extent a country is dependent on others where the following are concerned: *Technology, Cereals, Oil* and *Population* (see his forthcoming *Patterns of Dependence*).

In the field of 'development', population growth and communal land tenure
are both regarded in isolation from the socio-economic forces as a hindrance
to economic development, whilst population control and reform of the communal
land-tenure system are proposed as prerequisites to economic development. My
interest in population growth and land reform lies in questioning these
underlying assumptions.

The 'Problem' of Population Growth[14]

The rapid rate of population increase taking place in the so-called
developing countries accentuates "the problem of growing poverty amidst
economic expansion . . . (and has made) population growth occupy a predominant
place among development problems".[15]

The 'population problem' stems directly from the theory of Malthus who
propounded that "population tends to outrun the means of subsistence, making
preventative checks to population increase desirable and ultimately positive
checks necessary".[16] The same argument is still being put forward but with
more sophistication. For example, at one level population growth is
presented as a 'world' problem. As such, every human being is held responsible for seeing that world resources are not depleted by wantonly contributing to the 'population explosion'.

The fear of a doomsday which is supposed to come about if the 'population
bomb'[17] is not defused in time has caused the Americans to go as far as
developing a timepiece which monitors the world population increase.[18]
Unfortunately, the same is not done for the rate of consumption of the world
resources, of which almost 45 percent of the entire supply of raw materials
is consumed by Americans and Canadians, who make up only 6 percent of the
world's population (Sauvy, 1975: 91). At the same time, it is hoped that

> . . . once the people of the United States understand that they, with
> 6 percent of the world's population, consume about 35 percent of the
> world's total resources, and yet in terms of economic assistance as a
> percentage of GNP rank 14th among the 16 developed nations . . . (they
> will not) turn away in cynicism and indifference (Robert MacNamara,
> quoted by Susan George, 1977: 55).

At another level of sophistication, population growth is presented as a
problem by using an 'economic' argument, which sees population growth as an
obstacle whose removal is a prerequisite to economic development. Hence,

---

[14]That it is a 'problem' is so taken for granted that there is a book titled
appropriately *The Population Problem* (J. Moorman and M. Ingram, eds.,
1975).

[15]T. S. Epstein, *Research Proposal*, unpublished, 1973: 1.

[16]As paraphrased by J. L. Fisher and N. Potter, 1969: 106. For the general
background of Rev. Malthus, see K. Marx, 1977, Vol. One, Part VII,
Chapter XXV: 578, footnote 2.

[17]For the justification of using such lurid terms, see Hauser, 1967: 13.

[18]Early in 1977 the clock monitored the 4 billion mark, a fact which in
itself made news headlines.

"growth of population must be restrained in future in order to bring about
a substantial improvement in per capita incomes" (Bose, 1969).[19] Referring
to Kenya, Berg-Schlosser (1970) states that "any further growth in population
is likely to result in a deterioration of the average standard of life".[20]

This argument gains some scientific respectability from being augmented by
population studies done by demographers. However, while much is attributed
to the findings and projections of demographers, they have yet to provide
proof that population growth *per se* is a hindrance to economic development
or that their population projections carry a high degree of reliability.

> "Population projections, from Malthus to those of the recent past, have
> been notoriously wide of the mark . . . and a few projections into the
> future. . . . are altogether a hazardous and uncertain undertaking"
> (Fisher and Potter, 1969: 107).[21]

Kenya's population is projected to grow to between 28 and 34 million by the
year 2000 (1974/78 *Development Plan*: 100). The lower projection will be
realized only if the fertility rate falls to half its present rate. Lars
Bondestam argues that if the population is not to exceed 28 million by the
end of the century, the projection assumes a continuous decrease in the
death rate of

> ". . . approximately 0.1 percentage point per 5-year period, from 14 per
> thousand yearly during 1970-75 to 10 per thousand yearly during
> 1995-2000. . . . Bearing in mind that the population will remain fairly
> young after 30 years (because about 35-40 percent are under 15 years of
> age), this means that the age specific mortality rates in Kenya will
> fall below the rates in most of the industrialized countries. Such a
> fast demographic transition is beyond any probability - even in Kenya.
> Thus, there must be some errors in the original projection . . ."
> (1972: 11).

The positive checks necessary to curb a rapid population growth as Malthus
advocated have materialized in the form of birth-control programmes. Sauvy
observes that birth-control programmes rest on a tripod of three fundamental
illusions:

> "(1) lack of knowledge about serious and possibly lasting troubles that
>   arise when a population that has been growing fairly rapidly has
>   its growth stopped within a fairly short period;
> (2) illusions about the possibility of spreading the practice of birth
>   control quickly among a poor and illiterate population;
> (3) viewing the population of the world as a whole, when it is
>   heterogeneous and divided into independent nations" (1975: 71).

In this study, instead of dithering with figures on population increase and
population projections, I concentrate on why people want and need children
(Chapters 8, 10 and 11).

---

[19]As quoted by Epstein, *loc. cit.*

[20]*Ibid.*

[21]For example, between 1935-1944 there was a total of nine population
projections on the population of Britain by 1970. The projection nearest
the actual figure was 8 million off the mark (see Cox, *Demography*, 5th
edition, 1976: 261, Table 14.4).

I also demonstrate the vacillations of official population policies. For
example, from the late 1890s to 1910 the colonial policy was to settle the
'thinly populated' country with incoming Europeans; then came the native
reserve policy designed to squeeze plentiful cheap labour on to European
farms; and finally, the current policy which regards the rapid growth rate
of the population as a hindrance to economic development.

Land Reform

With the country's economic development based primarily on agriculture,
'modernization' has been regarded as impossible without reforming the
communal land tenure system. Basically, land reform is concerned with

> ". . . changing the institutional structure governing man's relationship
> with land (and this) involves intervention in the prevailing pattern of
> land ownership, control and usage in order to change the structure of
> holdings, improve land productivity and broaden the distribution of
> benefits" (IBRD, 1974: 1-3).

With the communal land-tenure system seen as an obstacle to good successful
farming, its reform into a freehold private individual land-tenure system
is regarded as a prerequisite to agricultural development.

> One of the requisites of successful farming is a system of land tenure
> which encourages investment in the land and enables it to be used as a
> negotiable asset. Traditional forms of land tenure inhibit this . . .
> (Development Plan, 1974/78: 59).

These ideas were succinctly voiced in 1954 (the year the reform became
official policy) by the then Assistant Director of Agriculture, Mr. R. J. M.
Swynnerton, when he published A Plan to Intensify the Development of African
Agriculture in Kenya (henceforth to be referred to as the Swynnerton Plan or
just the Plan). The land reform envisaged by the Plan was to be made up of
two complementary components: tenurial and agrarian reform.

Tenurial Reform: Under this reform it was intended to bring about the
eradication of the customary land-tenure system, which is basically egalitarian as well as communal in nature. In its place, a 'modern' land tenure
system, which was to be individualist as well as private in nature, would be
introduced. The individualization inherent in the tenurial reform was also
intended to involve the creation of continuous blocks of land by consolidating
fragmented holdings, as well as the registration of these holdings and the
issue of title deeds to their owners, and the reform of the customary inheritance law.

Agrarian Reform: Under this reform it was planned to lift the ban on the
cultivation by Africans of cash crops such as coffee, tea and pyrethrum.
This would be followed by the introduction of 'high breed' cattle - that is,
the crossing of native breeds with exotic (European) stock. Finally, there
would be infrastructural development in the fields of communication,
especially expansion of rural road networks, finance (e.g. making credit
facilities available to farmers), marketing (e.g. the development of
co-operatives), water (e.g. the building of dams), education (which was to
have an agricultural bias), and lastly, technical assistance (including the
transfer of the technology of cattle-dip buildings, the development of
extension work corps and other advisory services).

The land reform involves a concurrent implementation of the two components just outlined. Implementation of just one or only certain aspects of both would not warrant it being termed a land reform as outlined by Swynnerton.

Altogether I regard the whole undertaking as a myth. I use the word 'myth' here to denote ". . . the whole world picture held by a social group, and the value system anchored in that picture" (Gould and Kolb, 1964). And as far as the land-reform programme is concerned, I regard as false certain justificatory assumptions.

Firstly, the land reform which is being implemented is more tenurial than agrarian, thus making it pertinent to ask if it ought to be referred to as land reform at all. There seem to be two reasons for the heavy emphasis on the tenurial component of the programme. The first reason is that it is relatively easier and cheaper in the long run to implement a tenurial rather than agrarian-biased reform for the simple reason that there is no need for further allocation of funds once a tenurial-biased reform is carried out. In contrast agrarian reform is a costly business, both in its capital outlay and its running costs. This is an important point, because it is possible to argue that Kenya's agriculture could be modernized by implementing an agrarian reform which in itself does not necessitate a concurrent implementation of a tenurial reform. Even the World Bank (1974: 18) points out that in "some instances there may be no need for land (tenurial) reform" in order to carry out an agrarian one.

The second reason why the land reform has a tenurial bias is because there is a belief, held particularly by those who are helping the Government finance the programme, that private property creates incentives for economic development and any agrarian programme which does not directly cater to this belief will not get the necessary financial support (Leys, 1975: 70-73). The World Bank, while supporting the tenurial reform, nevertheless goes on to lament its outcome:

> "Socially, the reforms have created a class of prosperous small holders. In particular, those that were already relatively well-to-do have profited, while the poorest smallholders and nomads have benefited much less from the reform . . ." (IBRD, 1974, Annex 11:67).

A second assumption which I question relates to the apparent success of the white-settler agriculture, from which the current agricultural strategy stems. This was due not so much to the freehold tenurial system, but rather to the monopolistic environment in which it was operating (see Chapter 3).

It is also a myth to assume that the mere creation of freehold tenure necessarily leads to increased agricultural productivity. In Chapter 10 I argue that the incentives which are supposed to be generated by such a policy have yet to be proved effective. I also show in Chapter 9 that in spite of individual land ownership, the majority of peasants are unable to produce sufficient food supplies for their own domestic consumption. This is not so much due to rapid population growth as to the socio-economic differentiation to which land individualization is contributing.

Finally, I show in Chapter 7 that it is a myth that land reform lends itself ". . . to redress the imbalance in land holding so that production from all areas can be expanded" (IBRD, 1973:10). On the contrary, far from equalizing land distribution, it further exacerbates inequality in the rural areas and helps to accelerate the creation of landlessness.

Study Outline

When I first settled in my field location in the Taita Hills of Kenya in
August 1974, I was struck by the apparent lack of a 'village'. The immediate
phenomenon which caught my eye was the hilly topography together with the
nucleated pattern of human settlement. Houses either nestled on the hill-
sides or on the valley floors of these interlocking hills. But there did not
exist a village possessing the characteristics associated with the ideal
model.

The absence of an easily definable village posed unexpected problems for me.
Eventually I decided to work within the smallest administrative unit, namely
the sub-location, in this case Sungululu-Shigaro Sub-Location (see Maps 1, 2
and 3).

Shigaro-Sungululu Sub-Location lies between the 3500-5000-feet contour lines
and is found inside the high potential zone (agriculturally speaking). With
a total area of 16.5 sq. km, it has a population density of 219 per sq. km
(or 352 per sq. mile). It rises steeply on its southern Sungululu side,
only to descend abruptly and rise again on its northern Shigaro side.
Nestled between these two anticlines is Wundanyi township, which is the
district's headquarters (see Map 5).

The sub-location is divided into two sub-divisions or *mitaa* (*mtaa*, singular),
which are separate and identifiable as Sungululu and Shigaro. In turn, each
mtaa is made up of a number of *vijiji* ('hamlets'; *kijiji*, singular), each of
which is made up of a number of households. Hence the two *mitaa* have the
following *vijiji*:[22] Sungululu includes Mlambenyi, Kwa Ngori, Kilili/Mwanda
and Ndonga; while Shigaro covers Chome, Kirema Mtukunyi, Sirienyi and Mswadi.

I used Sungululu-Shigaro Sub-Location as the core working area for my study.
In particular, it provided the basis for my 100 percent census data which I
used to compute the demographic indices in Chapter 6. However, I did not
confine myself to the micro-society within the sub-location, but ventured
out through observation and primary data collection so as to encompass the
inter-area ecological and socio-economic differences thus acquiring a wider
perspective. For specialized data, such as that used in Chapter 11 on
family planning, the area involved was the entire Taita Hills.

Research Methods: Having lived in the field for a total of almost two years
(between 1974 to 1976), one of the main research methods used in this study
was participant observation. Subsidiary methodological tools used for data
gathering included census-taking, questionnaires, interviews and case
studies.

---

[22]For the census the micro-society was technically the whole of Sungululu-
Shigaro Sub-Location minus three *vijiji*, namely Kirema, Sirienyi and Mswadi.
But this was compensated for by the inclusion of the two *vijiji* from the
adjacent Wundanyi Sub-Location, Kilera and Ruma. This was done because of
easier accessibility of the latter and the fact that to all intents and
purposes, all the *vijiji* included make up a single social and ecological
area save for the administrative organization. However, for the purpose
of this study I refer to the micro-society I studied at Sungululu-Shigaro
(see Map 1).

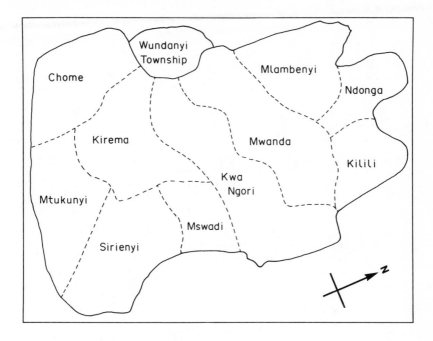

Map 1. Shigaro-Sungululu Sub-Location and its *Vijiji*
(Author's map)

A general census of the Sungululu-Shigaro micro-society was taken. Data
gathered in this way was used to provide the demographic indices in
Chapter 6. Questionnaires were both open-ended and closed. They were used
for obtaining information on food production and consumption, cash expenditure and family planning practices. Interviews were arranged in order to
augment the data on areas which were already under observation or inquiry.
Those interviews which were arranged tended to be formal, structured, but
nevertheless open-ended. Usually notes were taken or the interview was
recorded on tape. Other interviews were spontaneous, informal and
unstructured, and the information gathered was recorded as soon as the
opportunity to do so arose.

One or a combination of the methodological tools listed above were
incorporated in the gathering of in-depth data. I used case-study methods
of investigation to illuminate the following: labour utilization, food
production and consumption, cash expenditure, education, family planning
attitudes and practices. A non-random sample of sixteen households forms
the basis of analysis for all these topics with the exception of family
planning. I stratified the sample into four strata according to income, size
and quality of land owned and my personal knowledge of the socio-economic
conditions of the households involved.[23]

---

[23]In addition, the sixteen households were chosen because they formed the
most willing, co-operative as well as informative respondents.

This multi-faceted approach gives an in-depth picture of the dynamics of socio-economic differentiation in the rural areas. Its advantage is that it unfurls a particular social reality by showing the interplay of the different variables which contribute to the process of differentiation. This is unlike the mono-type case study, which is descriptive of a single past social reality. That is to say, it is centred on one unit such as an individual, a household or a phenomenon such as witchcraft or abortion. This 'mono' approach can help illuminate the case under scrutiny but often at the cost of distorting the social reality in which the case is located. It lacks predictive capacity because it attempts either to change or relate to the social reality so that the case can be accommodated.[24] Its explanatory power is due mostly to its descriptive exactness.

By taking a sample of sixteen households as a single case on the one hand, and within this sample treating each individual stratum as a case to be compared with the others, I hope to retain its applicability to the community as a whole, to give a picture that is real and relevant, thus reinforcing its predictive capacity.

For the more specialized data required for my chapter on family planning, I use the case-study technique to illuminate the attitudes of pregnant women towards child-bearing and the practices of contraceptive users.

---

[24]For an example of such a 'mono' case study, see "The Sociology of Sorcery in a Central African Tribe", T. Middleton (ed.), 1967.

PART ONE

The Taita

CHAPTER 1

The Setting

Taita[1] forms the main part of Taita-Taveta,[2] one of Kenya's forty-three administrative districts. It is one of six districts which together make up the Coast Province of Kenya (Maps 1 and 2). The District is situated in the western corner of the Province, extending between latitudes 3° - 4° South and longitudes 38° - 38.75^o East. On its north-western border lies Kajiado District of the Rift Valley Province, and on its northern border lie Kitui and Machakos Districts of the Eastern Province. Tana River and Kilifi Districts form the north-eastern and eastern borders respectively, while Kwale District forms the south-eastern border, all three districts being situated in the same Province as Taita-Taveta. Finally, it is bordered by Tanzania on its south-western and western sides.

The distinctive geographical feature of Taita-Taveta is the massive rise of the Taita, Sagalla and Kasigau Hills from the surrounding semi-arid plain called *nyika* - meaning 'the wilderness'. It is the Taita cluster of hills which dominates the rest in terms of surface area, population and altitude. The highest peak in the District, Vuria, which is over 7000 feet above sea-level, is located within the Taita Hills.

The District's topography, together with its altitudinal variations, allows it to encompass different types of climatological zones with their concomitant land uses and potentialities. This has led the authorities to categorize the agricultural potentialities of the District into three zones.

---

[1]Taita is the Swahili version of the local name Dawida. The people who live in Taita are called Wataita (Mtaita, singular) and they speak Kitaita. Hence Taita, Mtaita, Wataita and Kitaita are the Swahili versions of Dawida, Mdawida, Wadawida and Kidawida respectively in the local dialects. Wadawida means, literally, "the people of the mountain tops" (Harris, 1952). I use the Swahili versions in this study.

[2]Taveta, the smaller part which together with Taita forms the District, is separated from Taita proper by a 50-mile stretch of Tsavo West National Park. Immediate neighbours are Upare, Usambara, Chagga and Mt. Kilimanjaro across the border in Tanzania.

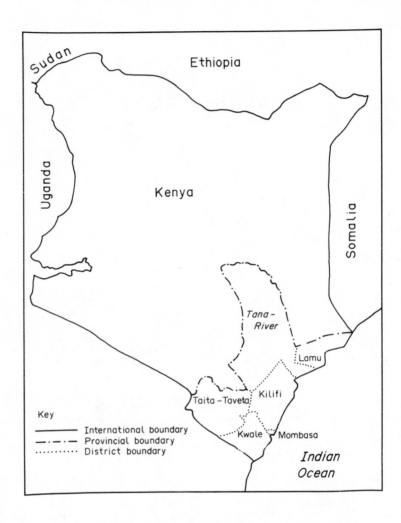

Map. 2. Kenya Outline Map with the Coast Province of
Kenya and its Districts.

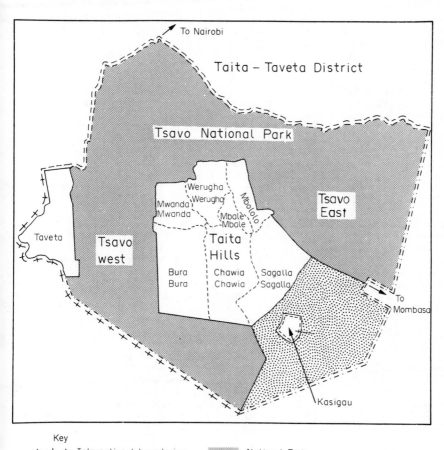

Map 3.   Taita-Taveta District.

The Lower Zone land is situated less than 2000 ft above sea-level. It has an average rainfall of not more than 20 in. annually, although there are areas above the 2000 ft contour with a similar low rainfall. Most of the streams which start from the hills become intermittent in this zone because of the long periods of hot, dry weather. The vegetation consists mostly of acacia, thorn-trees (known locally as 'wait-a-bit') and a thin cover of short, tough grass.

The Lower Zone is a thinly populated area, but it is teeming with wild animals. Part of the Tsavo East and the whole of the Tsavo West National Parks are situated in this zone.

Despite the good soil, peasant agriculture is difficult to practise because of the long spells of dry weather. Traditionally, the area has been used for hunting and cattle grazing within the Taita agro-economic system. The Government has recognized the Zone's potential as a grazing area and since the late 1960s has parcelled out chunks of land[3] to 'progressive' farmers for beef ranching, either as individuals, as a company or as a group.

Equally important to cattle grazing is charcoal burning. With a ready market not only in the urban areas, but also as far away as Dhubai and other Arab countries, the local people have persisted in cutting down trees for charcoal production, thus hastening the desertification of the area.[4]

The District's three sisal estates, namely Mwatate, Voi and Taveta, are located in the Lower Zone. There are also deposits of limestone and iron ore, not to mention valuable gemstones such as rubies and red and green garnets, which are commercially exploited both by the Government and private individuals.

The Middle Zone lies between the 2000- and 3500-ft contours. It has an average rainfall of 35-40 in. Compared to the Lower Zone it has better vegetation cover, mainly composed of shrub trees and tall grasses. In places the top soil is thin and sometimes rocky. Agriculture is handicapped by the fact that either the land is not high enough to catch adequate rain from the rain-laden clouds, or certain parts are found in the rain-shadow areas.

The Middle Zone is more densely populated than the Lower Zone, and it was at the foot of the Taita Hills, within this zone, that missionaries first founded schools. Consequently, in relation to the District as a whole, a higher proportion of people from this zone are able to supplement their meagre incomes from subsistence farming with earnings from salaried employment.

The Upper Zone lies over 3500 ft above sea-level. It receives an average annual rainfall of over 50 in. With good fertile soil and adequate rainfall,

---

[3]This area came to be known as Crown Land, or State Land after 1963.

[4]The Provisional Commissioner has prohibited further charcoal burning, but without success. Indeed, there seem to be influential people involved in the business, as witnessed by a seizure at Mombasa Port of charcoal bags which were about to be illegally exported. However, the prohibition will continue to be ineffective as long as the people are offered no alternative.

the Upper Zone and Taveta.[5] can be regarded as the 'granary' of the District.
It is also a densely populated area.

Almost all the land is cultivatable except where it is too rocky or too
steep. Coffee is grown as a cash crop, and so are bananas, citrus fruits and
vegetables, which are taken by truck twice weekly to Voi and Mombasa to be
sold. Much could be done to improve this trade, especially at the
communication and organizational levels. Other food crops, including maize
and beans, are grown primarily for home consumption, but are also sold for
cash at local markets in times of apparent surplus after harvest.

Area and Land Utilization: According to the Taita-Taveta Annual Report 1976,
the District's total area is 16,947 sq. km,[6] and is composed of the following
categories of land use:

> 21.6 percent (3661 sq. km) forms part of the Tsavo East National Park
> (Lower Zone); 45.8 percent (7770 sq. km) forms the whole of Tsavo West
> National Park (Lower Zone); 22.9 percent (3877 sq. km) is former Crown
> Land, now State Land which is used for beef ranching (Lower Zone);
> 9.5 percent (1608 sq. km) is agricultural land (mostly Middle and Upper
> Zones); 0.2 percent (26 sq. km) constitutes township areas (all zones);
> and 0.02 percent (5 sq. km) makes up forest reserves (Upper Zone; and
> Lower Zone in Taveta).

Due to its geographical setting, 90.3 percent of the District's total area
is 'animal land'. Human settlement and agricultural activities are
concentrated in the remaining land area, giving an average density of 67
people per sq. km of agricultural land.[7]

The Agricultural Cycle[8]

The cycle has two main seasons: the rainy and the dry hot. The rainy season
is in two parts, the long and the short rains. The long rains start towards
the end of March and continue through to June, May being the wettest month.
Then there is a spell of coolish dry weather lasting through July and August

---

[5]Altitudinally, Taveta falls within the Lower Zone. That it can be compared
with the Upper Zone in its agricultural productive capacity is due to the
fact that it has plenty of underground water coming down from Mt.
Kilimanjaro, and this has facilitated irrigation and enhanced its agricultural capacities, especially in banana growing and cotton cultivation.

[6]The District's area was given as 16,959 sq. km by the 1962 *Kenya Population
Census* (Vol.III, p.79) and as 17,209 by the 1969 *Census* (Vol.I, p.21).
However, all calculations in this study will be based on the 1976 figure.

[7]Using the 1969 population figures as a basis, and taking an annual growth
rate of 3.5 percent, the District's population was estimated to be about
128,379 in 1975, giving a density of 77 people per sq. km of agricultural
land - an increase of ten people per sq. km within a period of 6 years.
See *Urban Population Projections During 1969-2000 Within the Context of
Urban Development Strategy*, 1974: 23.

[8]This cycle is most applicable to the Taita Hills proper, which is where
most of the District's human settlement and agricultural activities are
concentrated, and where this study is based.

before the short rains, which come in September and October. The dry hot
season starts in November and continues without interruption up to March or
mid-April. The peasants use this season to prepare their *shambas* for planting
at the onset of the long rains.

Each rainy period has its base crop. In the Taita Hills, *maharagwe* (red
kidney beans) is the base crop for the long rains, while maize is for the
short rains. These two crops are the main foodstuff ingredients. But there
are other crops which are cultivated simultaneously either on the same plot
or on a different one. Vegetables such as cabbages, tomatoes, lettuce,
spinach, onions, carrots and potatoes are usually planted on separate plots
in the same *shamba*. These are basically cash crops and are grown all the
year round in irrigated plots in the wetter Werugha valley. In the lower,
drier areas they are usually multi-cropped or grown separately during the
long rains. Pulses such as cow-peas are multi-cropped with maize. Bananas
and sugar-cane, being perennial crops, are grown in the valleys.

Agriculture depends very much on the amount of rainfall, since there is little
irrigation being done due to the topography of the hills. As a result, one
frequently watches water flow by while crops on the hill slopes are withering
for lack of water.

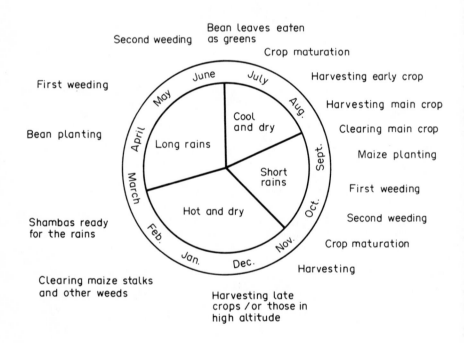

Diagram 1.1. Schematic Representation of the Agricultural
Cycle.

The People: The District's name could mislead one into thinking that there
are just two ethnic groups living in it, namely the Wataita and the Wataveta.
In fact there are four identifiable ethnic groups in the District, the other
two being the Wasagalla and Wakasigau, who live in the Sagalla and Kasigau
Hills respectively. These last two groups are usually regarded as Wataita
because of their close linguistic and physical proximity to this dominant
group. Together, the indigenous population makes up 90 percent of the total
population of the District. Of the indigenous population, the Wataita proper
make up the large majority, approximately 80 percent.[9]

Kitaita is said to have two major dialects: Kidawida and Kisagalla.
Kikasigau is regarded as a micro-dialect within the Kidawida dialect because
of its cultural and linguistic affinities (Nurse and Phillipson, 1973).
While from the linguistic point of view there are therefore only three ethnic
groups, for day-to-day purposes the Wakasigau are nevertheless considered a
separate group, and this is borne out particularly in time of crisis.[10]

The Kidawida dialect of the Kitaita language is spoken in the main cluster
of the Taita Hills. Within the Hills the speakers claim that there are
sixteen identifiable micro-dialects spoken in all.

Having located Taita and its immediate neighbours in the context of certain
important factors such as ecology, land area and its utilization, and having
briefly outlined the infrastructure of the District, I now turn to an
investigation of the origins of the Wataita and traditional society in pre-
colonial Taita, with special emphasis on its social institutions *vis-à-vis*
the land-tenure system.

---

[9]For the population figures of the respective indigenous groups, see p. 73

[10]During the First World War the Wakasigau, as an ethnic group, were
regarded by the colonial government as German collaborators and were
deported to Malindi in Kilifi District, to be allowed back to Taita-Taveta
(though not to their previous homes) only after the war (Bostock, 1950).

CHAPTER 2

Traditional Society

The present-day Wataita have developed out of culturally diverse bands of migrants who moved into the Hills at different times and from different places. The arrival of the first migrants is estimated to have been between A.D. 1300-1400. These first migrants are said to have found that the Hills were already inhabited by a pygmy people "which were divided into three clans referred to as the Wanyamba, the Wakuruma and the Wambisha" (Bostock, 1950: 5).

The inhabiting of the Hills by the ancestors of the present-day Wataita is part and parcel of that historical African phenomenon commonly known as the 'Bantu Diaspora' (Ogot and Kieran, 1968). The same process that can be seen in the movement of the Bantu-speaking peoples in their settling of most of Sub-Saharan Africa (West Africa excluded) is replicated on a smaller scale when looking at the origins, movement and pattern of settlement of a small 'tribe' like the Wataita (Spear, 1977).

With different proto-Wataita bands of migrants moving into the Hills at different times and almost certainly from different places, it cannot be said that the Wataita have a common place of origin. Present-day elders among the Wataita have a number of diverse claims of their origins. These claims locate ancestral origins as close as Ukambani, Maasai, Mwangea (Kilifi District), Usambara, Chagga and Upare, and as far as Elementaita (Rift Valley). Ethiopia, Egypt and even Israel and Portugal have been mentioned. Liszka (1973) not only shows how 'tribally' intermixed the early Wataita were, due to the various origins and stages of their ancestral arrival, but also how these people kept intermixing by constant movement and marriages once they were settled in the Hills. It is this dynamic fluidity within the Hills which forged a community with a sense of common identity and territory — the Wataita.

Social Organization

The Wataita are organized in clans, *vichuku* (*kichuku*, singular), of which there appear to be eight.[1] In fact, the *vichuku* play a minor role in terms of the social cohesion of members. Indeed, there are few people who can recount the names or the exact number of the *vichuku*. They are 'clans' in the sense that they give the order of immigration into the Hills by the proto-Wataita bands. Their sequential movement is always recalled during the *mlagui* ritual or divination,[2] when the names of the *vichuku* are intoned by the ritual practitioners. Each *kichuku* is symbolically regarded as an 'ancestor' in itself. However, because the people were given umbrella-like names to denote their order of entry into the Hills, this does not necessarily mean that they were organized on a clan basis at their places of origin.

Each *kichuku* is supposed to occupy what corresponds to the present-day location or sub-location of its descendants. But this is difficult to reconcile with conflicting information obtained from different sources regarding the origins and localities which the members of each *kichuku* are supposed to occupy, as Charts 2.1 and 2.2 show.

The amorphousness of a *kichuku* is only made less so by the way the term is also used to show how close people are related. Thus within the *kichuku* there is the *kichuku cha kavui* (minimal lineage) and the *kichuku cha kula* (maximal lineage). The minimal lineage has a depth of three generations starting from the *ego*. It is an exogenous social unit, which under Taita patrilineal inheritance law allows male cousins to inherit from one another. On the other hand, *kichuku cha kula*[3] is endogamous with a depth of seven to ten generations. Its size varies, but with an upper limit of about a thousand people, occupying a neighbourhood of about 3 square miles.

The term *weni* denotes the patrilineal lineage segment which runs through both the *kichuku cha kavui* and the *kichuku cha kula*. It is a term which is used at the segmentary peer level. Thus the descendants of Mwakivingo in the sample geneological chart on page 25 would be referred to as '*weni* Mwakivingo' by their first and second patrilineal cousins, the descendants of Mwasi as '*weni* Mwasi', and so on. At the next level, the descendants of Nyambu would be referred to as '*weni* Nyambu' by Mwacharo's descendants, who in turn would be '*weni* Mwacharo'. All the descendants of Mwakulegwa would be known as '*weni* Mwakulegwa' in relation to more distant kin or 'outsiders'.

---

[1]Different informants give different numbers, but eight *vichuku* seems to be a constant figure after cross-checking the different sources of information.

[2]This is a ritual involving the use of a goat's intestines either for fortune-telling, or explaining a misfortune or for passing judgement, as in cases of witchcraft accusation.

[3]Harris (1952) calls it *kichuku kibaha*.

Chart 2.1. Reconstruction of the *Vichuku* and their Origins

Vichuku*	Origins (listed by source of information)[†]			
	Chome	Mkumbo	Kiwinda	Liszka
Wasadu	Maasai			Kamba, Galla, Mwangea
Wanya		Ethiopia		Elementaita, Egypt, Usambara
Wasanu	Wahaya	Mijikenda	Mijikenda	Pokomo, Kamba, Shambala
Wasasadu	Israel			Upare, Mwangea
Wanyanya	Maasai			Kamba, Galla
Waikumi				Maasai, Kamba
Wambisha	Portugal			
Wanyamba	Taita	Taita	Taita	Taita

*The *vichuku* names are here listed in order of their supposed entry into the Hills according to the information found in a pamphlet written by Rev. Bishop Mwang'ombe, called "Kitaita Traditions and Practices" (unpublished). The last two *vichuku* listed are said to have been found in the Hills by the first six; and the last *kichuku* listed, the Wanyamba, is said to be the remnants of the pygmy clans Wakuruma and Wanyamba, who were poisoned by the Wasasadu, who gave the former a drink called *Ludi*.

[†] (i) David Chome (teacher),
(ii) Shedrack Mkumbo (peasant),
(iii) The late Rev. Jeremiah Kiwinda,
(iv) Stanley W. Liszka.

There were other informants, but their information was found to tally with one of the four main informants.

Chart 2.2. Reconstruction of the *Vichuku* and their Current Localities

Vichuku	Present-day localities (listed by source of information)			
	Chome	Mkumbo	Kiwinda	Liszka
Wasadu	Kishamba (Chawia)	Kishamba (Chawia)	Isi	Mwanda, Sagalla, Kasigau
Wanya	Wundanyi/ Werugha	Wundanyi/ Werugha	Wundanyi/ Werugha	Mgange Dawida, Sungululu, Wundanyi/Werugha
Wasanu		Sagalla		Kasigau, Mnanu, Mbololo, Shigaro
Wasasadu	Wumari	Wumari, Kasigau, Mbale	Shigaro, Werugha, Mwanda	Shigaro, Mbale, Wumari, Msau, Pusa, Rong'e, Mbololo, Kasigau, Kajire
Wanyanya	Paranga		Ngerenyi, Irizi, Nyache, Shaga	Mbololo, Irizi
Waikumi	Ruma		Ruma, Wesu	Mrugua, Bura, Mwanda, Mgange Nyika
Wambisha	Unknown			Disappeared
Wanyamba	Found throughout the Hills, though few in number			

It is this patrilineal lineage segment which today's Wataita refer to as
'clan'. And when asked to give their clan, the descendants of Mwakivingo
(Chart 2.3) might reply *'weni* Mwakivingo' or *'weni* Nyambu' or *'weni*
Mwakulegwa', depending on how far back they can remember and the relationship
of the actors. Rarely will today's Wataita refer to their *vichuku* directly.

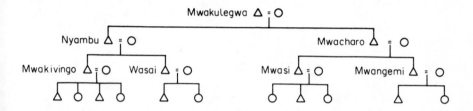

Chart 2.3.   A Sample Taita Genealogy.

Villages have been the traditional residential pattern of settlement. The
people lived in villages of varying sizes "consisting of a lone house
standing in the midst of gardens, in areas of poor soil and steep slopes ...
to closely packed assemblages of hamlets which may total more than two
hundred houses" (Harris, 1952: 9). With endogamy allowed within the *kichuku*
cha kula, starting from the fourth generation backwards, neighbourhood unity
and community identity were thus reinforced by interlocking relationships
based on marriage, residential pattern and other variables such as the agro-
economic system, which together were explained and justified through the
cultural idiom and community life.

Community Life: The Taita way of life, through its various expressions,
taught the individual the imperative of living communally, respecting age and
sex differentiation. Hence the people lived in villages, shared their meals
and cultivated their *kichuku* lands or those lands which they claimed by right
of first occupancy. The people pooled their cattle so as to graze them
together on the *kichuku* grazing lands on the *nyika*, the plains of the Lower
Zone. The herdsmen, who came from different villages, took turns in
collective herding, which was one of two major components of the agro-
economic system and invariably done by men (although it was the women's job
to remove manure from the stockyards at each changeover in the herding rota).
The other major agro-economic component was the cultivation of food crops,
which was (and still is) considered to be the work of women.

Squabbles at all levels - individual, family, village and *kichuku* - did of
course exist, but they were dealt with openly at public gatherings, where
conflicts were always regarded as detrimental to the community's cohesiveness
and were therefore resolved with this in mind. Even today attempts are made
to sort out squabbles such as witchcraft accusation or petty thieving in
this way, although not always with success. Many changes have taken place
which have undermined the basis by which the society legitimized its communal
existence.[4]

---

[4]Many other societies have also had their communal basis undermined. The
Wagiriama is one such example, as D. Parkin has observed in his book, 1972.

Running through this traditional socialization process, which emphasized collective rather than individual well-being, is an egalitarian ethos. This ethos was perpetuated in two ways. Firstly, Wataita were discouraged from being acquisitive at the expense of others.

> "There is an informal balance sought between the self-interest which Wadawida consider to be the mainspring of most human action, and joint responsibility. Community opinion is against the person who devotes much time and effort to openly acquisitive activities, and against people who indulge in conspicuous consumption, and most especially is this true when the offender is a son who grows prosperous while his father remains poor" (Harris, 1952: 13).

Two deterrents existed for the potential offender: his father's curse and/or being bewitched. Indeed, teaching aimed at curbing individualistic tendencies by threatening a parental curse or bewitchment is not limited to the Wataita alone. Parkin (1972) found that among the Giriama, regardless of one's economic status, there is a need for ritual practitioners who can divine and cure. Demand for protection against malevolent sorcery was higher among the upcoming entrepreneurs than among their relatively deprived community members. The instilment of fear into potential property accumulators in order to dissuade them from their acquisitive tendencies is not found in African societies only. In medieval Christian European societies the fear of being condemned to an everlasting hell fire was used for the same purpose as "evil witchcraft' in African societies – to control the acquisitive behaviourial tendencies of the community's deviants (Cohn, 1957: 169). In both societies the deviants have managed to free themselves from fear by adopting strategies to cope with it. The African seeks protection by fortifying himself with more powerful defensive sorcery; while the European has successfully transformed the egalitarian ethos embodied in his religion through a process of rationalization which creates a supportive ideology for acquisitive accumulation.[5]

A second aspect of socialization can be seen in the day-to-day pattern of living among the Wataita. This is also a process of reinforcing an egalitarian outlook in the people. For example, important property like cattle was the focal point of a number of individual interests within the group. While an individual could own a cow, this did not stop other people from claiming certain rights over it. A woman had the right to take the milk from her husband's cow. Men had the right of disposal, but only after consultation with his sons and wife (or wives if it was a polygynous family). The milk belonged to the herdsmen when the herding was done communally on the *nyika*. Moreover, herding and grazing was done on communally owned land. Above all, this egalitarian type of life was clearly defined in the agricultural land-tenure systems of the Wataita.

The Agricultural System: According to its use, land was divided into three major categories: Firstly, *nyika* (wilderness), which was used for herding and grazing jointly owned herds of cattle. In addition, since the *nyika* was teeming with wild animals, the Wataita could supplement their meat diet through hunting. Honey, for beer-brewing and eating, was procured by keeping bee-hives on the *nyika*.

---

[5]See J. M. Yinger, 1961, especially Chapter IV: "Calvanism and the Rise of Capitalism".

Secondly, *mlamba*, which was uncultivated virgin land to which every member
of the community had access and could enjoy a number of specific rights over
it, such as firewood collecting, grazing and the cutting of grass for
thatching. *Mlamba* was 'owned' by the *kichuku* living nearest it although
fundamental rights, such as disposal and cultivation rights, were exercised
by individuals in accordance with the land tenure system of the community.

Finally, there is the *mbuvha* which is a farm or *shamba* as it is known in
Kiswahili. These farms could be found in *nyika* and *mlamba* land, the main
distinguishing feature being that both cultivation and inheritance rights
were combined and bestowed on the head of a family, the process of which will
be dealt with in succeeding pages. The *mbuvha* formed the basis of the
family's livelihood.

Ideally, the *mbuvha* was composed of three land zones: high, middle and low.
The reasoning behind this was based on recognition of the hilly topography
of the country and its influence on "the availability of water, type and
quality of soil, and amount of rocks and boulders, as well as general
suitability for certain crops" (Harris, 1952). In addition to this, the
practice of polygyny and the traditional male-female division of labour were
factors to be taken into consideration. Nazoro (1974) argues that a man was
more assured of the constant maintenance of his farms and the production of
food supplies if he could station his wives on farms situated in the
different ecological zones or on multiple fields in one zone. With the men's
socially defined agricultural labour role limited to the preparation of land
for planting and the construction of irrigation work, he had a great deal
more spatial mobility than his wife or wives. This allowed him to become
involved in other activities such as hunting, bee-keeping and, most important
of all, cattle-herding.

A *mbuvha* situated in the high zone generally had soil of poor quality. This
zone was therefore primarily a grazing zone. The middle zone had good soil
for the cultivation of crops such as maize, cassava, sweet potato, millet,
kidney beans and other pulses. It was in the middle zone where the place of
residence was usually situated. The lower zone had wet soils, found mostly
at the bottom of river valleys, ditches and irrigated areas. Permanent crops
were grown here, such as two kinds of *midodo* bananas, sugar cane (for beer-
brewing) and arrowroot. Since it was difficult to find all three of these
land characteristics in any one *mbuvha*, it was necessary to have several
mbuvhas situated in different places and zones. Out of this necessity
emerged the practice of simultaneous cultivation of scattered *mbuvhas*, with
an inbuilt bias towards shifting cultivation.

Shifting cultivation was not therefore aimed at spreading risks only, but was
also a convenient by-product of the agricultural system. It is not always
appropriate to argue that the practice of shifting cultivation rested on the
availability of an inexhaustible abundance of land. In the case of Taita,
shifting cultivation, combined with simultaneous cultivation of scattered
mbuvhas, gave depth to the system as a whole. Shifting was done within a
defined ecological zone which was able to support a particular crop or crops.
Given the fact that some land had to be left at intervals to regenerate
itself, this system had the added advantage of spreading the reciprocal
benefits of access to land.

Thus, for instance, a man might lend a plot of land on which he grew one crop to a neighbour who could make use of it to grow another crop, or grow the same crop if the land has been left to regenerate itself for a long time and the 'owner' had other plots of land to cultivate. Such practices also helped to mitigate the growth of landlessness.

The farming system of the Wataita categorized land according to its potential use and 'ownership'. The more productive the land was, the more 'bunched' were the rights to it. These rights were technically permanent with regard to crops but not with regard to the land itself.[6] Thus, for instance, even when a *mbuvha* had permanent crops such as bananas or sugar cane, the owner of these crops might find himself obliged to allow another person to cultivate the same land, as long as the latter grew only non-permanent crops like maize or pulses.

In conjunction with shifting cultivation, which in itself was adaptive to the hilly topography, the Taita farming system reflected the land-tenure system.

Land-tenure System

Uncultivated Land: Land for the Wataita was the embodiment of their temporal and spiritual needs. Thus the land-tenure system did not attempt to isolate the economic aspect of land, but rather located it within their socio-cultural body-politic. Land was revered, not piously, but because it formed the socio-economic and cultural basis of Taita.

On the spiritual side, land was set aside for different types of protective shrines. There were the *seso* shrines, which were the grave sites of homicide victims who were regarded as being unjustly killed. Their grave sites became a source of spiritual worship and sacrifices. There were also *seso* grave sites which were not worshipped. These were the burial places of criminals, such as proven thieves and sorcerers. Whatever the type of *seso*, no one was allowed to build or cultivate on such land.

Then there were the *fighi* shrines. At the macro level, these shrines were supposed to protect the land from enemies such as the Maasai. At the micro level, they protected individual villages and property found within the villages. At this level, shrines could be moved from place to place whenever the people changed their residential area. Thus it was not the land itself that the *fighi* shrine occupied which was important, but its function, which was to protect the land.

It was the duty of the elders who were responsible for the *fighi* shrines to see also that the land was used to the best advantage. It was they who divided the land for cultivation and decided what land was to be set aside as *mlamba*, which provided pasturage, grass for cutting and woodlands for firewood collecting. In addition, land was set aside for market- and meeting-places, dancing arenas and paths. The elders were also responsible for organizing the community during famine by leading the people through prayer and attempting to discover any mis-use or non-use of land.

---

[6]This concept is more developed in Taveta, where the council of Elders (*Njama*) encourage outsiders to come and 'make the land productive'. The land would revert automatically to the *Njama*, to be given to another person for cultivation if it remained uncultivated due to the original cultivator's absenteeism or any other reason.

Apart from the shrines, forests were also revered. Prayers for rain were offered in forests which were specifically left uncut for this purpose. Land surrounding water springs and river banks, where there was invariably dense tree cover, was also sacred, and hence this land and its vegetation was preserved.[7] Also sacred was the land around the caves where ancestral skulls were kept.

Thus the Wataita apportioned certain land for particular functions which served the spiritual good of the whole community, this being a prerequisite to the exploitation of the land for the temporal needs of the people. It was where the cultivated land was concerned that pertinent questions as to who 'owned' the land and how it was distributed have to be asked.

Cultivated land: The land belonged to the Wataita as a community. Within this community, land was subdivided along the lines of the residential ridge pattern of settlement, each *kichuku* occupying its own cluster of ridges.[8] The individual came to 'own' land through his social position and relation-ships. 'Ownership' was defined within the context of social relationships, with land being inalienable. The concept carried an element of exclusion, that is, it was concerned with the rights between persons in relation to land, but not with rights of a person over land. Hence a man without social relationships was a man without land.

The social structure guaranteed the individual the use of certain rights over specified plots of land, but at the same time it expected him to surrender individualistic 'ownership' rights over land once acquired. The rights guaranteed the individual were two-fold: disposal rights and use rights. It was the use rights which were most important, and these included the rights of cultivation, firewood collecting, water fetching and the gathering of weeds such as *mnavu* and *munyunya*.[9] Ownership of land could be measured only by an individual's degree of control over disposal and distribution of use rights, especially for cultivation. These powers were invariably invested in men, the Wataita being a patrilineal society.

In traditional Taita society a man could 'own' land in one of four ways - first occupancy, purchase, conquest or inheritance.

With 'First Occupancy' land was owned by the individual who first cleared it. He had the power to distribute use rights to his family members as well as to more distant kin and members of his *kichuku*. But through his position as the first to occupy that land, it was subsequently a natural extension of *kichuku* lands. He could not therefore dispose of it by selling, for instance, without the consent of his immediate *kichuku cha kavui* members. To do so

---

[7]With the new individual land tenure most of the hills, springs and streams are nowadays cleared of their tree cover thus contributing to lower precipitation. The Government is now obliged to tell the peasants not to cut down trees, and indeed is setting an example by implementing an affore-station policy.

[8]The cluster of ridges which made up the *kichuku* land corresponds to what is now a location, of which there are six: Werugha, Mbale, Chawia, Bura, Mbololo and Mwanda.

[9]These weeds grow wild and are a source of vegetables in the diet of the Wataita (see pp.105, 106).

would be regarded as the most unforgivable anti-social behaviour, the more so if the buyer was from another *kichuku*. 'Land Purchases' were rare; the sale not in the way we understand the word 'sell', which connotes a willing seller and a willing buyer, a one-to-one relationship. The selling and buying of land in Taita involved a wider network of relationships, without which a transaction might be considered not binding by the community. A Mtaita sociologist[10] says that although

> "there is a system of buying and selling . . . I choose to term (this) as an extension of the granting rights system. I hold so because these rights . . . could be withdrawn on refund of the cost-price. Since land was foremost family, clan and people's property, no one ever went without rights to utilize it, and transactions such as selling were never privately done" (Mashengu, 1975: 3).

Indeed, it was necessary for the seller to ensure the support of his son or sons, otherwise the whole transaction could lose its meaning if the son or sons were to repudiate it. Acquiring land through 'conquest' is not a phenomenon of the recent past, but took place already during the migration into the Hills by the proto-Wataita. It was largely through inter-*kichuku* warfare that the present-day territoriality occupied by each *kichuku* was settled. No individual could unilaterally acquire land through conquest.

It is nevertheless known that not so long ago the Wataita used to go to war against the Wamaasai, Wapare and Wachagga (Bostock, 1950: 35-37; New, 1971: ch.15). The skirmishes between the Wataita and the Wamaasai were, from the former's point of view, for defensive purposes only. On the other hand, the Wataita organized raiding parties to Usambara, Upare and Uchagga. These raids were not motivated by expansionist policies but were for acquiring booty, which was mostly livestock or captives, especially women and children. Captured women and children were easily assimilated into Taita society. The women were married and the bridewealth paid to their 'captor', while male children were integrated into the *kichuku* and allowed to marry.

Inheritance of land in both monogamous and polygamous marriages was arranged by succeeding generation through male children after the death of the father. In a monogamous family, land and other property such as cattle were shared equally among the sons, with the last son's share included with the widow's fields which she was to cultivate until her death.

Inheritance in a polygynous household was patrilineal through matriarchy. Each son received an equal share of the land his mother held. The size of land each co-wife was apportioned depended on her marital seniority. The first wife received the largest share, the second wife the second largest share and so on. With the death of their husband, the widows became the trustees of the land and in effect played the late husband's role in allocating land and distributing the various rights to land within their matricentral domestic units.

---

[10]Mashengu wa Mwachofi has done research in the Mwanda Location of Taita in an attempt to find out the reasons behind the people's resistance to land reform. His unpublished paper is called "Land Consolidation in Mwanda Location: Agents of Change and Relationship to the community".

The preceding pages outlined the four ways in which a Mtaita came to "own" land; ownership here meant the ownership of a *bundle of rights to land*, which was made up of two interrelated aspects: *use rights* and *disposal rights*. Below I describe separately, what these rights entail.

Use Rights: While the use of land for cultivation stands out as most important, it should not be forgotten that there were other important ways in which land could be used, such as grazing and firewood collecting. What should be borne in mind is that a plot of land involved not just the 'owner' and his household members, but a wide network of relationships. Thus, while an individual might 'own' and cultivate a certain plot of land, it was nevertheless recognized that other members of the community could have access to fetch water, collect firewood or graze their cattle in the uncultivated part of the land. In other words, the concept of 'trespassing' did not exist.

The distribution of use rights was invested in men only, although a woman could act as 'trustee' during widowhood. In contrast, it was the women who utilized these rights most, especially the right of cultivation. A woman's accessibility to a plot of land depended on her marital status, as noted above.

Disposal Rights: The ultimate source of disposal rights was invested in the society as a whole.[11] The society was the *de jure* owner of the land but *de facto* ownership devolved downwards. It permeated through the *kichuku cha kula*, then the *kichuku cha kavui*, and finally down to the individual family head.

Rights of disposal were exercised by males of the society only, and inherited through the male line. However, while the men had control over the land through the exertion of these rights, this apparently *de facto* ownership of land did not give a man unrestricted powers over it. Cutting across the disposal rights were the use rights. The interaction and coalescence of these two types of rights resulted in communal land ownership through the social institutions of family, lineage and *kichuku*.

Ownership of the 'bundle of rights' might mean two things. Firstly, with regard to the disposal rights, it meant creating a landless group based on sex as a determining variable. Hence all women in Taita, denied disposal rights, were *de jure* 'landless'. Secondly, both married and unmarried sons could also be *de jure* landless before the deaths of their fathers. But both of these situations were counterpoised by the distribution of use rights which assured everyone access to land.

Access to land through the distribution of use rights obliterated the element of landlessness among the female Taita population. The newly married couple remained in the parental household up to the arrival of their second child. At this juncture, the young father was given a portion of land by his father for his wife to cultivate. He was allowed to have his own household, and could choose whether or not to be part of the parental residential unit, especially after the birth of their second son. This option was given to all sons except the last. After his marriage, the last son would remain as part of the parental residential unit but not necessarily as part of the consumption unit. He cultivated his parents' fields and automatically inherited them after his parents' death.

---

[11] This might be considered a widespread concept. For instance, in British law the Crown is the source of all title in land (see Sorrenson, 1968).

The system operated a little differently where a polygynous family was concerned. The man divided his fields among his wives and allowed them to cultivate in turn on a particular field if it was one on which every wife had her eye. Land was usually distributed fairly, ideally so that each wife's *mbuvha* included the high, middle and low ecological land zones. The man also kept some land for himself; either he cultivated it by himself, or he made his wives and children contribute some of their labour to his land. There was no standardized pattern in the utilization of labour in a polyga-mous domestic unit, for this depended on the husband's management of his household. His land served as a kind of insurance against the failure of crops grown by his wives.

Sons' wives in a polygynous family cultivated the fields of their respective mothers-in-law. A daughter-in-law was part and parcel of her mother-in-law's matricentral domestic unit, both in the productive and consumptive aspects. In polygynous families the young couples were also allowed to set up their own household after the birth of their second child. As for cultivation, the mother-in-law had to extend cultivation rights over part of her land to her daughter-in-law. The same pattern was followed up to the last son and his wife, who, even after the birth of their second child, in most cases continued to live in the residential place of the man's mother as part of her domestic unit, the young wife continuing to cultivate her mother-in-law's land.

While daughters inherited nothing from their families, they nevertheless enjoyed the same use rights to land as their male siblings before they got married. After marriage, they could still enjoy their cultivation rights over their father's land through the custom of gift-giving. By this custom, a father could give as a gift a portion of land to his daughter for her use. He would do this perhaps if his son-in-law had little land or if the latter's land lacked one of the three important ecological zones. Land given to a daughter as a gift automatically reverted to her brothers for inheritance after the death of their father, although her cultivation rights could still be continued until the death of her mother. At this point, she would have to make a new deal with her brothers, otherwise her cultivation rights would cease and the land be shared among her brothers. A daughter's cultivation rights could be extended to her children if there was no land scarcity on her brothers' side. This extension had no limit, although it was known to whom the land rightfully belonged, which was important if their offspring were to quarrel over it later on. The solution to such a quarrel would be determined partly by the manner in which the sister initially came to enjoy access to the land, in other words, whether it was through her mother, father or married brother (Harris, 1952: 16). If it was through her mother then the land belonged to her maternal uncles and their offspring. In fact the land would therefore be the property of another *kichuku cha kula* or of another *kichuku* altogether, since her mother had probably been granted cultivation rights by her father through the gift custom and in turn the mother had extended these rights to her married daughter.

The same would apply even in a polygamous family, with the major exception that the land reverted to a married daughter's brothers after the death of their mother, assuming that the portion of land the latter had given her daughter as a gift was part of her mother's inheritance from her husband. In this case the land was the property of her husband's *kichuku* whose heirs were her sons and not her daughters.

If a married daughter obtained access to land from her father, then this land belonged to her brothers and their offspring. In the absence of brothers, then it would go to the immediate male next of kin in her father's *kichuku*. On the other hand, the land was the property of her nephews if she initially obtained use rights over it from her married brother.

Hence, the phenomenon of landlessness was obviated by the land-tenure system. Nevertheless, the inheritance pattern had the potential for creating fragmentation of land holdings under certain conditions, such as in a free-hold individual tenure system and/or in the event of population increase. In addition, with inheritance passing from father to son, and social differentiation based on sex, male dominance over the society was thus reinforced and culturally determined.

Inheritance through the male line and virilocal marriages are just two of the customs in Taita society which show a bias towards male domination. Sons learnt prescribed socio-cultural roles which emphasized their higher status in contrast to that of daughters. Parent-son interdependency showed itself in concrete situations. Thus a son would inherit from his parents, be married by them, provide old-age security for them and perform their last burial rites.

The traditional Taita custom afer one's death was the exhumation of the corpse's skull - generally about two years after burial and after consultation with diviners. When the diviners had given the go-ahead, the son (or sons) of the deceased held a feast to celebrate the transfer of the deceased's skull from the grave to its final resting place, which was the *kichuku* cave where the skull joined those of other ancestors. In the case of those whose skulls were not exhumed, either there were no male children or perhaps the son(s) were too poor to pay for such a ritual.

According to Taita religious beliefs, graves and caves where skulls were placed were places of worship and veneration. But the physical movement of the skull from the grave to the cave denoted the deceased's social mobility upwards; that is, from being a mere deceased to being a spirit. It was also a movement which bridged the gap from being alone in a cold grave to joining a spiritual community in a warm cave. Every member of Taita society wished to reach this stage after his death, and a surviving male child was a guarantee for dying a 'hopeful' death.

The following Taita traditional story illustrates the importance attached to having a male child.

Once upon a time, there was an old man who lived on the *nyika*. This old man had two daughters and a large herd of cattle, but he had no son who could inherit his wealth. One day, one of his daughters was seduced by a hyena and subsequently she became pregnant. She gave birth to a son, but being ashamed of her action, she decided to hide her child under the protection of the hyena.
The second daughter became curious after noticing her sister's full breasts and a systematic pattern of disappearing in a certain direction after every meal. One day she followed her sister stealthily. Not far away from home, her sister sang a song and to her amazement she saw a hyena emerge from the bushes with a child. The hyena handed the child to her sister who suckled it and then gave it back to the hyena. After many months, the second sister decided to play a trick on the hyena. She went to the same spot and sang the same song. Immediately the hyena handed over the child to her. With the child in her arms, she

ran back home and gave him to her father. On seeing that it was a male
child, the old man was so thrilled that he called his daughter and
congratulated her for having provided him with an heir.

This story shows that having female children only does not provide a general
sense of security, since girls are regarded as 'transients' within a family.
Secondly, with the hyena being the most despised animal in Taita mythology
the story stresses the importance of having a male child and the
inconveniences people are prepared to put up with or steps they are prepared
to take to get a son. In the story, it is significant that the sexual taboo
relating to pre-marital sex and hence illegitimate children, is ignored.

The 'accumulation' of male children was through polygyny (Mkangi, 1975).
From their statements as well as from observation, it is clear that some
women saw a polygynous marriage as running counter to a woman's individual
interests in having the man to herself. If, say, she were to have only
daughters, the presence of co-wives who had given birth to sons could be a
painful reminder of her own inability to produce a male child for her man.
On the other hand, if she failed to give birth to a son in a monogamous
marriage, then she had the ever-present threat of her husband turning
polygynous. For the woman in a polygynous marriage, sons offered not only a
double security but also in certain cases a sense of autonomy which she
could not get in a monogamous family.

Thus, while to the Wataita all children were 'God's gift', male children
were more highly valued. This was due to the way the society functioned.
Male dominance was justified culturally and reinforced by the patrilineal
system of inheritance according to which men distributed property among
themselves.

We now turn to an analysis of the social, economic and cultural forces of
pre-colonial Taita society and how they were assimilated, preserved or
adapted in colonial Kenya.

PART TWO

Colonialism and its Legacy

CHAPTER 3

The Coming of Colonialism and the Settler Economy

The ivory and slave trades had managed to extend the Wataita's knowledge of a world larger than their own and had started to integrate them with it even before the coming of the missionaries and colonialists (Quiggin, 1949; Gray and Birmingham, 1970; Ogot and Kieran, 1968). However, it was these last two external influences which together were responsible for shaping present-day Taita.

The Missionaries

The Church Missionary Society (Protestant/Anglican) was the first Christian sect to start its prosetylizing mission in Taita-Taveta District. The first mission was founded in 1883 in Sagalla and the second was started in Taveta in 1892. Expansion into the Taita proper was not to start until 1900 when a mission was started at Mbale followed by a second one at Wusi in 1905.

However, it was Roman Catholic Holy Ghost Fathers who were the first to open up a mission station in the Taita Hills. They founded their station at Bura in 1892 and, until recently, most of the expansion has been around the immediate neighbouring areas of Bura, Mwanda, Mgange Nyika and Mgange Dawida.

The missionaries' major aim was to convert the people to Christianity. However, they experienced strong resistance. It took the Sagalla station almost 17 years to baptize its first group of Christians. In fact this breakthrough was achieved only after the people had suffered two devastating famines in 1889 and 1894 (known as the *mchango* or *mwakisenge* and the *kibaha* famines respectively). These famines enabled the missionaries to show their organizational skills in combating such calamities. And in so doing they managed to impart their Christian teaching through famine relief (Madoka, 1950: 4).

Going hand in hand with religious teaching was the training in literacy and craftsmanship, such as carpentry and masonry. Schools at the mission stations were started as 'Divinity Schools', which later on were to become primary schools with a bias to technical education, one such school being the Taita Vocational School at Wusi, started by the Rev. V. V. Verbi. Complementary to education was the missionaries' work as rural doctors. Armed with quinine

and other medicines, the missionary stations became focal points for the
local community through the medical service they offered.
Thus, through the missionaries' ability in providing such services,
Christianity fast gained popularity, the more so with the advent of
colonial rule.

The Coming of the Colonialists

Colonial rule came to Taita-Taveta through the Imperial British East Africa
Company (IBEAC), which obtained a royal charter on 3 September 1888. "With
the help of Mathews, whose services were lent by Bargash,[1] the Company's
headquarters were established in Mombasa; an advance post was set up at
Machakos, treaties were concluded with Nyika, Kamba and Taita tribes, and
preparation made for the 'effective occupation' of the interior" (Bostock,
1950: 11).

The interior became the East African Protectorate (EAP) on 13 June 1895,
under the British Government. On the same day the British Government
declared its intention of protecting this part of Africa and also of building
the Uganda Railway, Uganda having been declared a Protectorate a year before
(Sorrenson, 1968: 10).

The building of the Uganda Railway offered an incentive which led to the
'effective occupation' of EAP. The railway was built for strategic military
purposes - not to defend the EAP and Uganda Protectorate, but to defend
Egypt, which was important strategically for the defence of British India.
Otherwise, there was no locally based commercial or political advantage to
justify the building of the railway. The economic advantages to be gained
through such a railway once built, however, were easily recognized by British
Chambers of Commerce. Sorrenson writes that the Lancaster Chamber of
Commerce "wanted British intervention to open new markets for British goods"
(1968: 10).

The search for markets for British manufactured goods was, then, the 'silent'
driving factor behind the building of the railway. The 'noisy' factor was
the strategic one. This was easily understood by the British 'public', whose
support the British Government needed if it was to launch a project as
ambitious as the Uganda Railway (Sorrenson, 1968: 10).

The railway reached Kisumu on 10 December 1901. Once completed it took on a
life of its own. It had to pay for its existence but was unable to do so
for several reasons: one of these was that for the first 300 miles it passed
through thinly populated areas, which meant that there was no immediate
market for British products, as had been hoped by the British Chambers of
Commerce. In addition, the railway took longer and was more costly to build
than expected, the major reasons for this being the absence of a detailed
survey before construction, the lack of reliable financial estimates before
1900, a year before it was completed, and the inhospitable climate and
difficult terrain. Further factors were the non-cooperation of Africans and
hence the importation of a labour force from India, and the costly wars
carried out against the people's resistance to British occupation, especially
along the railway line.[2]

---

[1] Seyyid Bargash was the Sultan of Zanzibar. Zanzibar was the launching pad
for activities like the slave and ivory trade, exploration and military
expeditions into East African hinterlands.

[2] Between 1897-1913, 68 percent of total expenditure in the EAP was devoted
to military purposes (see Wolff, 1974: 50).

The construction of the railway had fortuitously increased the value of the EAP, and since the running of the Protectorate was a burden on the British taxpayer, some way out had to be found. The railway was seen as the key to providing a solution to this problem. It had to be made to pay; the question was, how?

The Coming of the Settlers

Westward from Nairobi, the railway passed through some of the best agricultural land in the Protectorate. For the most part the area had an elevation of over 4500 ft above sea-level and an annual rainfall of not less than 30 in. Its elevation gave it a temperate type of climate which was regarded as suitable for European settlement. To quote Sir Harry Johnston:

> "In the Eastern part of the Uganda Protectorate there is a tract of
> country almost without parallel in tropical Africa: a region of perhaps
> 12,000 square miles, admirably well watered, with a fertile soil, cool
> and perfectly healthy climate, covered with noble forests, and, to a
> very great extent, uninhabited by any native race. This area lies at an
> altitude not less than 6000 feet and not more than 10,000 feet. It is
> as healthy for European settlers as the United Kingdom, British Columbia
> or temperate South Africa. I am able to say decidedly that here we have
> a territory (now that the Uganda Railway is built) admirably suited for
> a white man's country" (Ross, 1927: 46).

Prior to the coming of European settlers and their effective occupation of this part of the Protectorate, which they later called the 'White Highlands', many programmes had been considered to make this land agriculturally productive. Attempts were made to make the Protectorate the America of the Indian sub-continent. Recruiting missions were sent to Punjab to entice prospective settlers, but without success (Wolff, 1974: 61-52; Sorrenson, 1968: 34). The highlands were even offered to Zionist leaders as a possible Jewish homeland, but the offer was turned down (Sorrenson, 1968: 31; Ross, 1927: 65).

The idea that the land be settled by Europeans received a boost in 1901 with the arrival of Sir Charles Eliot as the new Commissioner of the Protectorate. With gusto and dedication he embarked on a programme which would entice European settlers into the country. He sent emissaries to South Africa to offer the vanquished 'Irreconcilables' - the Boers - what would be for them a new frontier after their defeat in the Anglo-Boer war. In the meantime, there was a constant flow of settlers arriving from the U.K., New Zealand, Australia and Canada, thus giving by 1906 a European population totalling 1814 (Wolff, 1974: 53).

The British settlers within the European population wielded much more power and influence than their number warranted. Among them was a group of "aristocrats like Delamare, Hindlip and Cranworth, or gentlemen adventurers, like the ebullient E. S. Grogan" (Sorrenson, 1968: 67). This group of aristocrats and adventuring settlers formed, as it were, a vanguard pressure group which was bent on pushing for European interests. To achieve this, they fought for the control and ownership of the main productive resource - land. Constant pressure was put on the Protectorate Administration and on the Foreign and Colonial Offices in London, with the result that a land-tenure system was introduced which was conducive to their interests, at the expense of the indigenous African population.

The Settlers and the Land: As Wolff has said, "the first demand of the settlers was for the exclusive land rights for Europeans in the Highlands" (1974: 55). This led to the demand for the right to unrestricted land-grabbing, which inevitably resulted in land speculation, both at individual and company level. On this score, it is worth noting that as early as 1907, Lord Delamare had over 100,000 acres of land, while a company called East African Syndicate had 320,000 acres (Ross, 1927: 73).

The settlers took for granted that land was the property of the individual. What they were interested in was to get the most favourable terms of owner-ship from London and the Protectorate Administration. For example, they attempted to introduce in a 1909 Land Bill a 'perpetual quit-rent' clause which, if passed, would have introduced "a tenure under which the land could be held, if the rent was duly paid, in perpetuity" (Ross, 1927: 73). The failure of the Bill did not stop the alienation of land from the Africans by the settlers. By manipulating the Crown Lands Ordinance, the settlers dispossessed the Africans of their land with active support from the local administration. After some hesitation, London finally allowed the settlers to own land on a lease that was extended from 99 to 999 years (Wolff, 1974: 61-67). Under the Crown Lands Ordinance of 1915 and the Kenya (Annexation) Order in Council of 1920,[3] any rights the Africans might have claimed over the land disappeared. Their lands now became Crown Lands and they themselves became "tenants at the will of the Crown" (Ross, 1927: 87).

Wolff argues further that the immigration of settlers into the EAP, later to become Kenya, was part of a grand British imperial design to protect "existing international economic relations, mainly those in India, and the speediest possible lessening of British dependence on extra-empire markets and sources of food and raw materials (Wolff, 1974: 146). It was the second objective that the country was designated to fulfil; and the settler migrants were chosen as agents of change. Conditions had therefore to be created to enable them to carry out their historic mission. Realizing the importance of their role within the structure of British imperial objectives, the settlers had from the start shown no qualms in pressing for their interests, whatever the consequences for the Africans. Such determination can be seen in the following quote of Sir Charles Eliot:

> "Your lordship has opened this Protectorate to white immigration and colonization, and I think it well that in confidential correspondence at least, we should face the undoubted issue – viz., that white mates black in a very few moves. ... There can be no doubt that the Maasai and many other tribes must go under. It is a prospect which I view with equanimity and a clear conscience" (Wolff, 1974: 66).

Indeed, the Maasai 'went under' with the loss of most of their land through treaties which they signed under pressure. With the 1904 treaty, they vacated the Rift Valley and moved to Laikipia in the north. The subsequent treaty of 1911 forced them to move back southwards to what is now the southern Rift Valley Province, an area they still occupy today (Ross, 1927: 132). Other societies which went under were the Kikuyu and Nandi, among others, of the Highlands, and the Mijikenda, Wataita and Wataveta in Coast Province (Sorrenson, 1968: 210).

---

[3] 1920 is the year that the EAP became the *Kenya Colony and Protectorate*. The Protectorate was a 10-mile coastal strip, administered by the British on behalf of the Sultan of Zanzibar, which also enjoyed Protectorate status.

The settler economy developed an agricultural system that was mainly orientated towards production for export. The system had two main sectors; ranching and farming. Within the farming sector, production was of two kinds: plantation and mixed farming. Plantation farming involved a mono crop type of cultivation, with one large farm given over to the production of a single crop such as sisal, coffee, tea or sugar-cane. Mixed farming included dairy farming together with the cultivation of cash crops such as coffee, tea, maize, wheat and other perennial crops.

With little adaptation, Kenya's agricultural system is still patterned in this way. Indeed, the large mixed farms are still regarded as the cornerstone of the country's economy, thereby qualifying for development funds amounting to K£5 million in the 1974-1978 Development Plan, just K£104 less than the amount set aside for the development of small land-holdings, and in spite of the fact that the former benefits a small minority in contrast to the latter. To understand such a contradiction, one must look at the self-perpetuating mechanism of the system.

As has been seen, right from the beginning the settler community had great influence over the colonial administration. Once they had used their influence to obtain land on the most favourable terms possible, they turned to the question of how best to develop this land through cheap labour. Africans were to be the source of this labour, and the settlers' function, according to the then Colonial Secretary, Joseph Chamberlain, was to oversee "natives doing work of development" (Wolff, 1974: 92). With this in mind the settlers wrote to the then Governor Sadler:[4]

> "We must point out, your Excellency, that it is grossly unfair to invite the settler to this country, as has been done, to give him land under conditions which force him to work, and at the same time to do away with the foundation on which the whole of his enterprise and hope is based, namely, cheap labour " (Wolff, 1974: 93-94).

Labour Recruitment Measures : In pursuit of cheap labour,[5] the following strategies were employed: the creation of Native Reserves, the introduction of taxes, the introduction of the *Kipande* system and the creation of Chieftainship.

Under the influential 1905 Land Committee, Africans were to be herded into 'native reserves', a strategy intended to kill two birds with one stone. Firstly, the physical removal of Africans into reserves and the confiscation of their livestock was intended to make room for incoming settlers (Sorrenson, 1968: 210-225). Secondly, by confining Africans to reserves whose land could support a limited number of people, it was envisaged that, with normal population growth, the excess population would be released into the labour market. The more the reserves were reduced in size, the more labour was squeezed out, for "the existence of unnecessarily extensive reserves is directly antagonistic to an adequate labour supply" (Ross, 1927: 92).

---

[4]In 1907 the king's representative was given the title of 'Governor' replacing that of 'Commissioner'. Sadler was both the last Commissioner and the first Governor.

[5]See Ross, 1927, Ch. VI: "Labour Troubles", which is interesting to compare with Huxley, 1953, Ch. 10: "Labour Crisis".

Taxes were imposed on Africans as early as 1902. In this year the Hut Tax
was introduced, levy being collected from each hut. This tax hit hardest
polygynous marriages, whereby a husband built a hut for each wife. To
protect themselves against heavy taxation people huddled themselves into
fewer huts. In 1903 Poll Tax was introduced to stop the tax-evasion tactics
adopted by Africans. Its basic provision was that every male over 16 years
of age was liable to be taxed.

The rate of taxation climbed from 2 rupees per person per annum in 1902 to
10 rupees by the 1920s. Thus by the early 1920s Africans contributed in
direct taxation £ Sterling 501,615, while Europeans paid £ Sterling 162,775
and Indians £ Sterling 46,790 (Ross 1927: 163).

In addition, indirect taxation through custom excise duty was introduced
after Lord Delamare's proposal in 1911 that imported commodities (these
included cotton pieces, blankets, salt, beads, etc.) consumed by Africans
should have their freight rates increased on the Uganda Railway.

While one of the aims of the taxation policy was to raise finances to run the
local administration, nevertheless the major goal was to compel the "native
to leave his reserve for the purpose of seeking work. Only in this way can
the cost of living be increased for the native, and . . . it is on this that
the supply of labour and price of labour depends" (*East African Standard*,
8 February 1913, quoted in Wolff, 1974: 99).

The creation of reserves and the introduction of taxes did not increase the
supply of labour sufficiently to satisfy the settlers' requirements.
Further oppressive and exploitative measures were instituted, of which an
archetypal example was the enactment in 1915 and subsequent implementation
in 1920 of the Native Reserve Ordinance No. 56, which introduced the *Kipande*
(Pass) system in Kenya.[6] The system required that every African male carry
a *Kipande* which showed his place of work, type of work, wages, the duration
of his employment and general behavioural characteristics. All these were
to be recorded by his employer.

Another step towards the provision of cheap labour was the creation of the
Chieftainship at the grassroots level. The Chieftain's important function,
with his assistant known as the 'headman', was to be a grassroots labour
recruiter.

Role of the Administration: While the Administration was under pressure from
the settlers, it would be true to say that the Administration also offered
their active support in the search for cheap African labour. In 1919
Governor General Northey issued a Circular aimed at mobilizing the entire
administrative machinery towards supplying enough cheap labour for the
settlers.

The Government offered services such as siting railway lines through European
farming areas. Roads built in European areas were financed by Central
Government grants, while those in African areas by taxes on African produce.
In addition, a rating system was introduced which allowed European-grown
maize, wheat and other temperate foodstuffs to be carried at a lower cost
in comparison to African-produced export crops such as cotton.

---

[6]The Pass system originated from South Africa, and Kenyan settlers did not
fail to see its advantages. See Appendix I for a sample of a registration
certificate used in the *Kipande* system.

The Administration also made available to the settlers a good number of efficient extension workers from its survey and veterinary divisions. The Agricultural Department established experimental farms, distributed equipment, seeds, seedling, livestock (all exempt from tariffs) and generally designed "all its activities to inform Europeans and improve their farming. ... It is no exaggeration to conclude that the quantity and quality of official assistance to European agriculture in Kenya were among the highest in any colonial experience" (Wolff, 1974: 88).

The settlers were also assisted by the Administration in their efforts to keep non-Europeans away from the White Highlands, except as labourers, servants and petty shopkeepers. Local administrators were discouraged from assisting Africans to produce export crops such as coffee, even under European supervision in the reserves (Lamb, 1974). Missionaries were likewise discouraged and indeed, they "took up land alongside settlers, under the same land regulations and adopted the same methods of cultivation" (Sorrenson, 1968: 257). Measures such as the imposition of an annual licence of 15 rupees on coffee farmers were further intended to serve as deterrents against African competition.

In summary, it can be argued that European agriculture was economically viable because it operated in a protected environment and hence could enjoy monpolistic advantages (Yoshida, 1971: 76-102). Leys (1975: 34) enumerates the following variables over which the settlers had a monopoly: the most fertile and productive land, the so-called 'White Highlands'; cheap agricultural labour; Government services, such as the siting of railway lines through European farming areas, and finally the most profitable crops, especially coffee.[7]

What, one must next ask, were the effects of this European monopoly on the African population and on African agriculture?

The African Population

It is estimated that the African population rose from 2 to 3 million in 1897 to 4 million in 1902 (Kuczynski, 1949: 144-148, 215). After reaching this peak, the population started to decline, levelling off at its lowest in 1921 when it was barely above 2 million. Although different sources give different figures,[8] what can be deduced is that within a period of two decades the African population declined by almost half from its peak of 4 million. It was almost back to its previous peak in 1944, two decades later, when the figure stood at 3,800,000 (Beck, 1970: 219).

The 1914-1918 war was one of the contributory factors of this decline. Africans were recruited into the East African Carrier Corps as well as into the Armed Forces. Out of a total number of 350,000 Africans directly involved in the war, 46,618 (13 percent) died. Of the dead, nine out of ten came from the Carrier Corps. This "appalling mortality among the African porters who accompanied the fighting troops and maintained the lines of

---

[7]The ban on Africans growing coffee, wheat and pyrethrum was lifted in the mid-1950s. For the after-effects of lifting the ban, see Lamb, 1974.

[8]Wolff, 1974: 107, Table 5:1 gives the figure 2,483,500. Kuczynski, 1949 (Vol. II:215) quotes 2,300,000, and Beck 1970: 219, Table 5 refers to 2,574,000.

communication was a failure of the campaign outstanding in its grim tragedy"
(Beck, 1970: 64). An example of such tragedy is a 24-week period in 1917
when a total death toll of as many as 68 people a day was recorded. Such a
high death rate was the result of a combination of contributory factors such
as disease (for example, malaria), poor food and arduous work, which might
involve, say, walking 15 miles while carrying a 40-pound load daily (Beck,
1970: 64).

The outbreak of famines - man-induced ones - also played a significant role
in the reduction of the African population. With the creation of the
reserves, the agro-economic systems of the people collapsed; that is, they
were marginalized[9] by the settler economy. This in turn led to famine.

There were famines in pre-colonial East Africa. But the difference between
pre-colonial famines and the famines of the colonial and post-colonial era
is that the former were mostly due to natural causes, while man-made factors
have contributed significantly to the latter. Wisner (1976: 6), quoting
Kjekshus (1973: 46-58), referring to the 1880s and 1890s, lists outbreaks
of rinderpest, smallpox, jiggers and locusts as the major causes of famine
during this period.[10] While the occurrence of famine due to drought was not
unknown in pre-colonial East Africa, the various African agro-economic
systems had adapted themselves to dry years through the growth of symbiotic
relationships between the different societies, manifested in trade and
through physical mobility. Hence we read that during the 1889 and 1894
famines which occurred in Sagalla and Taita, most of the food came from the
coast, from surplus-producing people like the Wagiriama (Madoka, 1950: 8-9);
in addition, people migrated to the coast or Taveta. The *makilambua* (rain-
seeking) Wakamba likewise settled on the coast during the 1830s drought
(Kimambo, 1970: 80).

The interdependent relationships and the freedom of movement were broken by
colonialism. The Wagiriama, who grew grain for export to Arabia as well as
for the up-country people, were reduced to subsistence farming when they were
forcibly moved from their land in the Sabaki River area and confined to a
reserve.[11] It is no surprise therefore that between 1915 and 1916 they
experienced famine (Leys, 1924: 127-128). The same dislocating factors
caused the Wakamba to suffer in 1924-1925 the first of their many famines in
the coming 50 years.

---

[9]Wisner describes a marginal person or household as one whose mode of
production has been seriously disturbed or destroyed by contact with the
capitalist mode of production, yet whose productive energies have not been
absorbed by the latter (1976: 1).

[10]Small-pox and jiggers, like rinderpest, were introduced or possibly
reintroduced by Europeans. Jiggers were introduced in 1980s probably from
Brazil via West Africa and the Congo, crippling much of the working
population in some areas (Kjekshus, 1977: 57-78). Zwanenburg and King add
chicken-pox, measles, poliomyelitis, plague, influenza, whooping cough,
relapsing fever and sleeping sickness (1975: 9).

[11]The Wagiriama resisted this move and fought the British in 1913-1915,
see Sorrenson (1968: 287-288) and Temu, "The Giriama War, 1914-1915" in
Ogot, 1972.

The settler economy succeeded in marginalizing the African agro-economic systems which manifested their downward trend in the form of famine. So it is now necessary to look more closely at the collapse of these agricultural systems.

African Agriculture

The disruption of African agricultural systems was the outcome of sheer exertion of the social, economic and political power which was inherent in the existence of 'settlerdom'. For the African, confinement to a reserve meant removal from more fertile and abundant land; where the reserves were large the soil was usually poor. Africans in reserves were also prohibited from expanding into better land, while access to essential resources such as water, salt licks and grazing pastures was either prohibited, restricted or difficult.[12] This meant that within the reserves the delicate balance between man and his environment was strained and adversely interfered with. In addition, intrinsic to the policy of creating reserves was the desire to keep Africans from easy reach of the lines of communication, which otherwise could have facilitated their active participation in the wider economy.[13]

With laws and regulations determining labour supply and market availability for agricultural produce purposely tailored and manipulated in order to exclude African contribution and participation, African agriculture had no other option but to remain at subsistence level.

The measures employed to guarantee a steady supply of cheap labour have already been outlined. What has not yet been made clear is that both the African and the settler agricultural systems reached their peak periods at the same time. Thus both systems also demanded extra labour at the same time; and since expatriate agricultural production depended on African cheap labour, the settlers were faced with the problem of labour shortages whenever the peak periods arrived because of the Africans' concentration of labour on their own farms. It should be noted, however, that Huxley (1953: 214) admits that "labour shortage was not due to any lack of able-bodied men (but rather) due to the fact that the average native did not want and did not need to work for Europeans". With the natural response by Africans concerning labour allocation and utilization having an adverse effect on European agriculture, labour laws were rigorously enforced in order to ensure an abundant flow of cheap labour to settler farms. Thus in many cases, this meant that the entire sources of labour of African households - men, women and children - were forced to abandon their farms at peak periods to work on those of the Europeans. This is just one of the many strategies which actively contributed to pushing African agricultural production to subsistence level and thus making the people more vulnerable to famine outbreaks.

---

[12]The Wakasigau were confined at Sembe and Vongoloni in the Lower Zone of Taita-Taveta District, where "women have bother in drawing water, and the goats have nothing to drink" (Chief Kisaka as quoted in Kenya Land Commission, 1934, *Evidence*, Vol. 3: 2746).

[13]White settlers in Zimbabwe (Rhodesia) employed the same policy in order to eliminate African competition (see Ranger, 1968: 278).

The conflict over labour utilization was also experienced whenever a new cash crop was introduced into African agricultural systems. A cash crop such as cotton, which required intensive labour at the same periods as food crops, inevitably proved to be unpopular with the peasants. For security reasons, they would rather have a sufficient food supply than cash. To an outsider, such an attitude might seem peculiar. It could also be regarded as an ideal example of the legendary peasant conservatism and lack of enterprise. But historically it is known that whenever force was used to make peasants cultivate a cash crop like cotton, which diverted labour from the cultivation of their food crops, they usually resisted - actively as in the *Maji Maji* rebellion in the then Tanganyika territory (Iliffe, 1969: 1-29), or passively by seeing that yields were kept low. Dumont (1957: 74-114) cites examples, recorded in West African societies when the people were forced to grow cotton, of yields of 120 lb per acre where there was co-operation and 53 lb per acre where there was resistance.

In Kenya, passive resistance by peasants to the dislocation of their agro-economic base by colonial and independent governments still continues. The Government laments this resistance in the following way:

> "The Government for a long time has placed high priority on increased cotton production, although rather little progress has been made. Demand on the world market remains favourable, and increased quantities are required by local processing industries. The problem is one of supply, not demand" (*Development Plan, 1970/74*: 236).

Since it was envisaged that the native reserves would serve as labour reservoirs for settler agriculture, they were intentionally limited in size. In some cases, instant demographic pressures followed the establishment of a reserve.[14]

The Taita reserve was established in 1905 and had an area of 198 square miles or 126,720 acres, comprising approximately 42.5 percent of cultivatable land, 37.5 percent of uncultivatable land, including rock, forest and precipitous slopes, 16.0 percent of grazing land and village sites, and 4.0 percent of roads and tracks, railways, rivers and swamps.

From 1925 to 1932 the adult population density in the Taita reserve rose from 78 to 98 per square mile. In 1933 the District Commissioner recorded a total population of 39,674, made up of an estimated 8695 families, who were to cultivate 53,856 acres. On average each family had 6.19 acres of cultivatabl land. The population per square mile of cultivatable land was 476 people.

There were other reserves which were more densely populated than Taita (Humphrey, 1947: 2-4). But what they all had in common was the impact of demographic pressure on an ever-decreasing man/land ratio due to rapid population growth from the mid-1920s. Demographic pressure shortened the fallow period inherent in shifting cultivation. Thus land was intensively exploited through the practice of overcropping and overgrazing, which in turn accelerated the process of soil erosion and exhaustion.

---

[14] In 1905, Nandi population density almost tripled from 23 to 64 people per sq. mile when 1250 sq. miles were alienated in the process of establishing a Nandi Reserve (Sorrenson, 1968: 214).

In this chapter I have attempted to show how Taita society had its links
with the outside world consolidated by different forces. I have shown how
missionaries, acting as the forerunners of colonialism, replaced its previous
links through the slave and ivory trades. Under the impact of colonial rule
Taita, as part of what was then the EAP, was integrated into a larger society
by the building of the Uganda Railway. I have argued that in this process
Taita and other societies were dislocated from their own régimes of development by an expanding capitalist system, mirror-imaged by the white settler
community.

The amalgamation of a number of individual societies such as the Wataita into
a larger Kenyan society was achieved at great cost to these individual social
entities. During the first two and a half decades of colonial rule their
populations were much reduced due to the concatenation of a number of factors:
their resistance to colonial rule; involvement in a foreign war; and man-
induced famines, which were both a cause and result of the collapse of their
agro-economic bases. Leys summarizes it like this:

> "Down to 1912-13, African production had accounted for at least 70 percent
> of exports. By 1928 it accounted for less than 20 percent, and from 1925
> absolute value of African export production declined as the reserves
> increasingly relapsed into subsistence farming to support their
> increasing populations" (1975: 31).

Hence by the 1930s the monopoly enjoyed by the white settler community had
successfully managed to underdevelop the African agro-economic base to
subsistence level. This decline was in itself shattering.

CHAPTER 4

The Underdevelopment of African Agriculture

While the previous chapter has shown how the African agro-economic base was marginalized by the penetration of a settler dominated colonial economy, this chapter addresses itself to the interplay of the various factors which culminated in the tenurial reform of the 1950s.

By the 1930s, the unproductiveness of African agriculture had become common knowledge to the colonial administration. As already mentioned there was a continuing decrease in the man/land ratio in the native reserves due to population growth. Reduction in the occurrences of 'pacification wars' and improved public health were, among others, contributory factors to this population growth. The result was land sub-division and fragmentation, which in turn aggravated soil erosion and soil exhaustion.

With the productive capacities of African agriculture marginalized to subsistence level, steps were taken to prevent it from reaching open starvation level. The African agro-economy was necessary for the survival of the settler economy because it provided cheap labour[1] as well as a market for manufactured goods. Hence ameliorative measures had to be taken to prop it up. Most of the recommendations were made by experts on economic nationalistic grounds. Non-economic justifications for such measures – for example, political – came to be recognized as the major motivating factors later, especially after the outbreak of the Mau Mau peasant war in Ukikuyu, Meru and Ukamba in the late 1940s and the declaration of emergency on 20 October 1952. Meanwhile, the dynamic process of underdevelopment which was taking place in the African reserves was attributed to rapid population growth, soil erosion and exhaustion, and traditional land-tenure systems.

---

[1]Apart from forced labour, labour was also cheap because of depressed wages. It was argued that, since Africans grew their own food by practising subsistence agriculture, there was no need to pay them higher wages commensurate to their jobs. This is one of the strands running through the 1950s and early 1960s 'dual economy' theory (see Boeke, 1968; G. M. Meier, 1964: 48-55; R. L. Meier, 1965: 44-47 and 59-61). There is still the tendency to use the dualistic theory with regard to the development of Kenya's agriculture, thus denying the holistic and structural linkages due to the historical development of this sector.

Concern about the destructive effects of these variables provided the water-
shed of varied administrative programmes which aimed at salvaging the African
agro-economic base. These programmes reached their peak in the mid-1950s,
when it was advocated that reform of African land-tenure systems was a
prerequisite to successful land reform in terms of improved subsistence
agriculture.

The Kenya Land Commission 1932-1934

The Kenya Land Commission of 1932-1934 marks the beginning of a long
programme which culminated in the transformation of African tenurial systems.
This transformation was to form the basis of the 1950s land reform.

The Commission was to operate within a framework consisting of seven terms
of reference (see Appendix II). Except for the sixth, which was to "define
the area, generally known as the Highlands within which persons of European
descent are to have privileged position in accordance with the White Paper
1923", all of the terms addressed themselves to problems appertaining to
Africans. But this did not necessarily imply that African problems carried
more weight as far as the Commission was concerned. Indeed, the contrary
was the case. Thus they recommended the legitimization of land already
alienated and potential land for further alienation for the use of a
European population which did not exceed 5000 (Soja, 1968: 21).[2]

In its final report, the Commission divided the country into three land
categories: sparsely inhabited areas, native reserves and 'the rest of the
Colony'. Out of the country's total 219,730 square miles (exclusive of
water), 63 percent of the land formed the sparsely inhabited areas with a
population density of 0.4 per square mile. The native reserves occupied
22 percent of the total land area, but carried 86 percent of the entire
African population with a density of 54 per square mile. The rest of the
Colony, which included the land settled by Europeans, occupied 15 percent of
the total land area and carried a native population density of 9 per square
mile.

The White Highlands were located in what the Commission referred to as 'the
rest of the Colony'. Its total area was 32,639 square miles, of which
10,345 (32 percent)[3] had already been alienated and a further 1530 (5 percent)
had been surveyed for alienation. Forest reserves occupied 4284 square miles
(13 percent),[4] unsurveyed Crown Land 15,649 square miles (47 percent)

---

[2]Soja 1968: 21 gives an estimate of the highest possible limit, i.e. of the
combined European and settler community. As for the settler community only,
Leys, 1975: 29 shows that it was more than 4000 even by 1953, having
alienated more than 10 million acres, although occupying only 7.3 million
acres. Quoting E. A. Brett (*Colonialism and Underdevelopment in East Africa,*
1963: 175), who was in turn citing the 1934 *Agricultural Census,* he says that
by 1934 there were about 2000 settlers only, occupying 5.1 million acres of
land.

[3]Soja says that of these 10,345 sq. miles, only 52 percent was cultivated or
grazed; 20 percent was occupied by African squatter-labourers and nearly
28 percent was unoccupied (1968: 21).

[4]Among other uses, the forests served to hold land for future European
alienation without the political embarrassment of having large extents of
unexploited land lying idle at a time when Africans were living in over-
crowded reserves (Soja, 1968).

and coast freehold, which together with townships and land for public purposes totalled 831 square miles (3 percent).

I have estimated that with a settler population of not more than 2000, their population density on the alienated land was about 0.2 per square mile. This works out at approximately 5.1 square miles or 3310 acres per settler. In contrast, the African in the reserves had a per capita average of 0.02 square miles or 12 acres.[5]

On the whole, the Commission recommended the expansion of the native reserves. Land for the use of Africans was classified as follows:

Class A: Native Lands, which included the existing native reserves, together with all additions to be made on 'grounds of right'.[6]

Class B1: Native Reserves, which was land recommended to be added to Class A land to fulfil certain economic needs, if these needs appeared to be permanent.

Class B2: Temporary Native Reserves, which like Class B1 land could be added to Class A, but only to fulfil a need which appeared to be temporary.

Class C: Native Leasehold Areas, which was land to be set aside for lease to natives on a private basis, and to non-natives when this was considered to be compatible with native interests.

Class D: Communal Reserves were areas in which natives were to have equal rights with non-natives in respect of acquisition of land (for the Taita Reserve, see Map 4).

The main factor which obliged the Commission to recommend the expansion of the native reserves was the high rate of increase of the native population. For instance, by the early 1930s, the Wataita's annual rate of increase was certainly not less than 3 percent. A study of 698 families by the Catholic Bura Mission recorded a declining infant mortality rate from 323 to 188 per thousand during the period 1924 to 1931, while the adult mortality rate was 20 per thousand per annum by 1928 (Kuczynski, 1949: 213-215).

The second factor behind the recommendation of expansion was the need to make their agro-economic base viable, and hence in the case of Taita, the Commission took into consideration the topography and its influence on the agro-economic system when it came to its recommendation. The total area of the reserve was doubled to 400 square miles. Additional land was incorporate from Class A and B2 land, with the majority coming from the latter. Only 81 square miles came from Class A. Of particular significance was the inclusion of an area of 2 square miles in Wundanyi, which was part of the Class A land.

---

[5]By present-day standards 12 acres per person seems to be a generous portion of land; as a statistical figure, it should be borne in mind that by no means all of the land was fertile and suitable for agricultural production.

[6]By 'grounds of right' it would seem that the Commission meant a territorial claim based on the irrefutable historical fact of first occupancy.

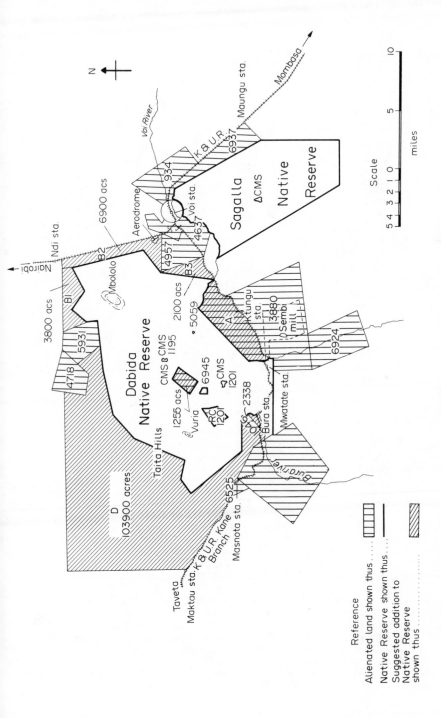

Map 4. Sagalla and Dabida Native Reserve.

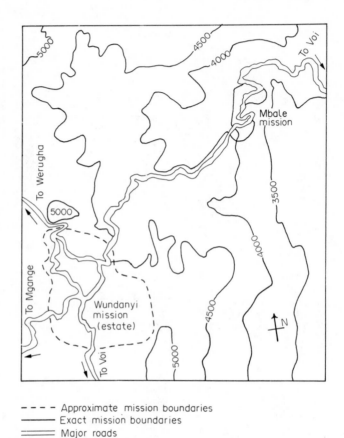

---- Approximate mission boundaries
——— Exact mission boundaries
════ Major roads

Map 5. An Enlarged Map of Wundanyi Estate.
(For the Estate's agricultural statistics, see Appendix 8).

These 2 square miles which make up Wundanyi, the present-day District
Headquarters, was given to the Industrial Mission Aid Society on a freehold
title basis in 1906. The Society transferred its title to East African
Industries Ltd., who in turn sold the land to Wundanyi Ltd. in 1916. In 1922
the land was leased for 10 years to a Major Drury, who attempted to grow
coffee with little success. When the Major's lease came to an end in 1932
(the same year the Commission was appointed), Wundanyi Ltd. decided to sell
the property for £5000 and gave first option to the Government. It can be
deduced from this that the Government agreed to compensate the estate owners
at the price they asked for, and the Commission was thus allowed to recommend
the estate's addition to the surrounding native reserve.

The remaining 119 square miles added to the Taita reserve came from Class B2 land. This land was to be converted to Class B1 as the natives' economic needs appeared to be permanent.

Class C land - 'Native Leasehold Areas' - was not added to the Taita reserve since it did not have squatter problems such as those found in the Kikuyu reserves. But whenever it was included into a reserve, in addition to alleviating the squatter problem, Class C land was expected to cater for the interests of three classes of persons:

"(a) Advanced natives in the Reserves who might be desirous of renting land which they could develop as private holding.
  (b) Returned labour-tenants from alienated areas, who, having lived for several years away from the control of tribalism, may find it difficult to be re-accommodated in their own Reserve, either through lack of room for themselves and their stock, or because tribal life is no longer congenial to them.
  (c) 'Detribalized' natives who are loosely attached to towns, and who should be removed from them and offered the alternatives of going to live in the Reserve with which they have most affinity, or taking up land in Class C areas, if they can afford to do so" (*Kenya Land Commission Report, 1933*: 370-371).

Here lies the genesis of the ideology of private property, the accompanying values and attitudes of which appeared as if they had grown spontaneously in the reserves. The introduction of the individual tenurial system later on was to be seen not only as a logical step but also to have some few supporters - in this case, in the form of advanced, returned labour-tenants and detribalized natives.

Soil Erosion and Exhaustion

Complementary to the Kenya Land Commission was the on-going policy of soil conservation. The official line was that soil erosion and exhaustion was caused by overpopulation, primitive methods of agriculture and overstocking.

The Land Commission had already attempted to solve the problem of over-population in their recommendation for expanding reserve boundaries. However, between 1939 and 1960, and under thirteen different schemes, only 11,024 people had been settled (Van Zwanenberg, 1975: 48). In other words, during a period of 21 years, an average of about 525 people were settled annually. Thus settling people into the additional lands was a slow process and did little to promote soil conservation.

The Administration introduced new methods of cultivation designed to improve existing farms and, at the same time to preserve the soil. To prevent further soil deterioration, projects such as hillside terracing, grass planting, grazing enclosure erection and river bank reinforcement were embarked upon. Having failed to persuade the peasants to carry out these measures voluntarily, the Administration resorted to coercion. The upshot was that peasants were forced to work 6 days in every 3 months on communal schemes. In some areas police had to stand behind agricultural inspectors to ensure the work was done. But this did not stem peasant opposition. In Ukamba, for instance, peasants threw themselves in front of tractors as the ultimate defiant gesture to these forced measures (Van Zwanenberg, 1975: 48).

Another measure taken by the Administration was the propagation of the policy of de-stocking. Van Zwanenberg argues that the policy was propagated ostensibly as a measure to combat soil erosion. In actual fact, it was yet another measure taken by the Administration to eliminate African competition with Europeans in the livestock trade.

From the onset of colonial rule right up to the 1940s, pastoralism was seen either as an impediment to settled agriculture, and hence development, or as an anachronism which ought to be left alone. Here I have in mind the growth of the 'noble savage' concept and the idea that 'tribal' life should be interfered with as little as possible. But such attitudes overlook the fact that the establishment of the European stock industry in the country initially relied on the supply of animals from African herds. These animals were obtained through confiscation during the so-called punitive expeditions at the onset of colonial penetration. For instance, in 1906, 11,000-12,000 heads of Nandi cattle were confiscated and auctioned. These cattle provided the supply for European herds and "as soon as Africans had provided the raw material for the European livestock industry, *great efforts were made to keep African and European animals apart*" (Van Zwanenberg, 1975: 93).

The main thrust behind livestock development was therefore aimed at supporting European ranching and discouraging African pastoral development. This was to be achieved even if it entailed the transformation of pastoral societies into sedentary agriculturalists. This transformation was clearly perceived by the colonial administrators. Van Zwanenberg quotes the then Nyanza Provincial Commissioner, C. M. Dobbs, who said with some perception in 1914:

"... it might seem as a gross piece of interference when we say that the native must be necessarily restricted in his pastoral tendencies. To such I distinctly state that the best interests of the natives are served when they are restricted in such inclinations and are practically compelled to take to mixed agriculture. Among all African tribes excessive pastoral proclivities more or less influence nomadic or unsettled conditions in their life" (1975: 93).

He was supported by the then Governor who, not to be outdone by his subordinate, said:

"... my policy is to discourage these pernicious pastoral proclivities by every legitimate means, not only because they are productive of nomadic tendencies but because they inculcate in the minds of the people a distaste for any settled industry" (Van Zwanenberg, 1975: 93).

The Kenya Land Commission expressed these same sentiments in its Report in this way:

"The proclivity to accumulate stock without regard to economic advantage is manifest among nearly all these tribes" (1933: 559).

Further steps taken to separate African from European stock were the declaration of Turkana and what was then the Northern Frontier District (now North Eastern Province) as 'closed districts' and the imposition of quarantine regulations which followed. The declaration was made for security reasons and maintenance of 'law and order' because of frequent incidences of cattle raiding among pastoralists.[7] Added to this, nomadic pastoralism was

---

[7] For the sociological importance of these raids see Van Zwanenberg, 1975: 80-90.

confined to demarcated 'tribal' grazing areas just as it was in areas where
sedentary agriculture was practised.

Restricting nomadic pastoralism to specified areas runs counter to the
economic essence governing this type of stock-rearing. The socio-geographical
ecology was tampered with, giving rise to further accumulation of livestock
as the only ultimate security within such a disrupted environment. Going
hand in hand with livestock accumulation was the increasing phenomenon of
soil erosion. For the nomadic pastoralist, denied easy access to markets
due to the quarantine regulations as well as the establishment of international boundaries, there was no alternative but to accumulate more livestock in case of prolonged severe drought or an outbreak of epidemics. To
the outsider, this rational socio-economic behaviour appeared to be
inexplicably irrational and it was dubbed the 'cattle complex'.[8] Henceforth,
pastoralists have been regarded as suffering from this 'complex' and unwinding
them from it has been taken as a prerequisite step towards 'modernizing' them.
Even when it was recognized that the so-called cattle complex rests on a
justifiable economic rationality, it was nevertheless a patronizing and
blundering recognition:

> "The Hamitic and Nilo Hamitic pastoralists had a genuine 'cattle complex'
> . . . based primarily on their retention as a form of insurance. . . .
> This complex might have taken much longer to break down but for the
> 1939-45 war in which so many of the young men from the pastoral tribes
> served (and) acquired a habit of meat-eating . . ." (Ministry of
> Agriculture, 1962: 5).

But a herd of cattle has significance beyond its economic function for the
de facto owner. To the owner, his herd

> ". . . is a complex organization of individuals tied to one another in
> diverse ways; quite as complex as the community of people he lives in,
> and in many ways reflecting that community. His herd reflects the
> household structure, the lineage, and the clan; expresses the network of
> social relationships as they extend to his father's father and the yet
> unborn son of his son. . . . *These considerations do not render him
> sentimental about the animals as such.* . . . Thus he will trade, give
> away, or slaughter his animals as circumstances demand . . . but in the
> final analysis, his herd is his autobiography and his monument; through
> it he will gain such immortality as may come to a Sebei herdsman"
> (Goldschmidt, 1976: 144-5; emphasis added).

Prior to implementing de-stocking measures, the colonial régime attempted in
the mid-1930s to create a market where African pastoralists could sell their
surplus animals. Liebigs, a Rhodesian private profit-making concern, was
invited to open a meat-canning factory at Athi River, a spot where Kamba and
Maasai stock routes meet. Other stock routes were organized so that animals
could be brought down to Athi River from stock-holding areas such as Samburu,
Kajiado, Narok, Kitui and Northern Frontier District, without passing through
European areas for fear of infecting European stock (Van Zwanenberg, 1975:
100-101). Liebigs was to offer a fixed price for the cattle and public
auctions were to be organized in the reserves, to operate within this price-

---

[8] It is pertinent to point out here that people in or coming from industrialized countries have not been dubbed as suffering from a 'money complex'
although they rely on money for survival, just as the pastoralists relied
on livestock animals.

controlled framework. But European stock-owners opposed this plan. What
they foresaw was the under-cutting effect of market forces contained in it.
Had the plan been put into operation, they feared that Nairobi butchers would
have gone to the reserves, offered to buy cattle at a price slightly higher
than that paid for 'European meat'. This possible loophole within the plan
would inevitably have encouraged African competition and thus threatened the
monopolistic hold enjoyed by the settler community. European stock-owners
supported the policy of de-stocking, ostensibly as a conservationist measure,
although in fact it was seen as a way of stifling African competition, whilst
at the same time ensuring a sufficient supply of stock at the Liebigs' canning
factory.

Liebigs' exploitative prices in effect acted as disincentives to African
participation in the scheme. The highest price they offered for a full-grown
head of cattle was 15 shillings, and for a sheep or goat, 2 or 3 shillings.
Outside Liebigs' market monopoly, a head of cattle fetched between 60 and
100 shillings, and a sheep or goat about 10 shillings (Van Zwanenberg, 1975:
101). To break even, the canning factory required a minimum of 40,000 head
of cattle a year. This supply was not forthcoming from the African stock-
owners for the reason already mentioned. On the other hand, European stock-
owners either had insufficient supply, or, even if they had not, they were
not prepared to sell their stock at the price Liebigs had offered to African
stock-owners. At the same time, it was uneconomic for Liebigs to buy all its
stock demands from Europeans because of the exorbitant price demanded for
European-raised stock. With African stock-owners unwilling to part with
their animals, the existence of their herds was more of a threat to the
European protected stock market than the aggravation of soil erosion. To
pre-empt this economic threat, European stockowners pressurized the colonial
régime to take stringent measures against the pastoralists.

Hence, in late January 1938, the Governor ordered the forcible confiscation
of Kamba cattle and by July of the same year 20,000 head of cattle had been
obtained and sold at Liebigs' price quotation (Van Zwanenberg, 1975: 101-102).
This policy triggered off strong opposition which culminated in a march of
2000 Wakamba to Nairobi where they "encamped near the Governor's residence
for about three weeks until the compulsory 'de-stocking' was dropped"
(Kimambo, 1970: 92).

De-stocking measures were implemented in other areas, such as Samburu and
Kamasia in 1939, but on a smaller scale. The whole problem of soil erosion,
which was seen as a consequence of overpopulation (hence overcropping) and
overstocking (hence overgrazing), and the official policies which were
embarked upon to cut the linkages within this vicious circle were abandoned
when the 1939-1945 war broke out.

So far I have argued that from the beginning of the colonial era up to the
1940s, the agro-economic systems of Kenyan societies were marginalized as a
result of the incursion of a capitalist mode of production, spearheaded by
the European settler community. I have also dealt with the disadvantageous
side-effects caused by the capitalistic settler economy on the African
economy, in contrast with the official diagnosis of the underdevelopment
process, and the (ineffective) strategies which were developed to counteract
this process. Official thought attributed the deteriorating conditions of
the native reserves to three factors, namely: rapid population growth, soil
erosion and exhaustion, and traditional land tenure systems. I have already
given an overview of the first two factors. In so doing, I have attempted to
locate both the official policies and the African responses within a socio-
economic environment created by the coming into contact of two different

modes of economic production, each propelled by its respective socio-cultural milieu. The following chapter deals with the last of these factors, the traditional land-tenure systems.

CHAPTER 5

Swynnerton and Traditional Land Tenure Systems

Before the 1930s, official thinking was directed towards the preservation of communal native land-tenure systems. Individual tenure was confined to the 'White Areas'. It was feared that if it were to be introduced into the native reserves, it would encourage the emergence of a landless unemployed group "who could start trouble'. However, from the 1930s onwards, communal land tenure came to be regarded as an impediment to agricultural development. The Land Commission wrote: "We regard a conscious advance towards private-holding to be generally desirable, if land is to be developed to the best advantage . . ." (KLC Report, 1933: 423).

The African Land Development Board (ALDEV)[1] regarded "African traditional forms of land tenure (as) *all too often incompatible with good farming*" (The Ministry of Agriculture . . ., 1962: 6; my emphasis). Prior to this, Swynnerton, author of the famous Swynnerton Plan, had this to say:

> "All the African lands in Kenya naturally suited to semi-intensive or intensive farming are already populated, some more, some less densely, suffering from low standards of cultivation and income and, *in particular as a result of African customary land tenure and inheritance* . . ." (1954: 9; emphasis added).

The same theme was taken up by the economic mission to Kenya sent by the World Bank in 1962:

---

[1]ALDEV was started in 1945 at the time when the Kenya Ten Year Development Plan 1946-55 was being prepared. It changed its name six times: it started as 'African Development Board' (1945-1946); then 'African Settlement and Land Utilisation Board - ASLUB' (1946-1947); 'African Land Utilisation and Settlement Board - ALUS' (1947-1953); 'African Land Development Board - ALDEV' (1953-1957); 'Land Development Board' (Non-Scheduled Areas, i.e. the native reserves) (1957-1960); and finally, 'Board of Agriculture' (Non-Scheduled Areas) (1960-).

"Land Tenure in the Non-Scheduled Areas[2] is much more complex because of
the variety of tribal attitudes to it. At one extreme are tribes which
control large areas of land which they regard, under customary law, as
common property, exclusive to the tribe as a whole, no tribal member
having individual rights in it. ... *Tenure of this nature is one of
the greatest obstacles to agricultural progress*" (The Ministry of
Agriculture, 1962: 47, emphasis added).

It would be false to assume that these arguments were developed in isolation
from what was happening in the native reserves. In the final analysis, it
could be argued that the 'economic' justifications put forward to maintain
or change communal land tenure depended on the Africans' actual or potential
response as measured within the general framework of colonial economic
development. African response was seen as a barometer, and policies had to
be a step ahead and be able to predict the response in order to maintain the
initiative embedded in the colonial socio-political *status quo*. Thus, for
example, as early as 1949 the District Officer of Nyeri (Central Province)
was urging the Central Government to "begin to temper the wind to the lambs
that are soon to be shorn" in anticipation of political agitation coming
from ex-servicemen, who were unsuccessfully to try their hand at becoming
traders (D. J. Penwell, quoted by Leys, 1975: 51, footnote 48).

Christianity and Formal Education: the only alternatives: Denied active
economic participation, Africans turned to formal education under missionary
guidance. The missionaries imposed their conditions before allowing Africans
to become Christians and hence the opportunity to become literate. They
imposed blanket conditions, branding anything to do with the African way of
life as uncivilized and therefore unchristian. Those Africans who abandoned
or denounced their 'traditional' way of life became 'Mission Boys' and were
the first group to be exposed to formal education. It did not take long for
Africans to recognize the importance of formal education as a tool of social
mobility and as a means of collaborating with or combating the colonial
régime. This recognition caused those Africans who could not agree to the
missionaries' terms to find other means of obtaining formal education. Hence,
whilst in Ukikuyu, the missionaries prohibited the practice of clitoridectomy,

> ". . . a large number of people broke away from the main Christian body
> and began to seek other means to satisfy their spiritual hunger without
> denouncing their social customs. Apart from religious sentiments, there
> was a general discontentment about the land question. At this time
> people who broke away from the missionary influence , together with the
> indigenous population, began to form their own religious and educational
> societies. The most popular of these are the Independent Gikuyu schools
> and Kareng'a schools, which combine religious and educational activities"
> (Kenyatta, 1938: 273).

---

[2]To remove the racial slur, the East African Royal Land Commission (1953-
1955) recommended that the terms *Scheduled Areas* and *Non-scheduled Areas*
were to be substituted for *White Highlands* and *Native Reserves*, respectively.
Hence, the Scheduled Areas comprised "the areas formerly reserved for
European farming and the Kibos-Miwani sugar growing area in Nyanza, a total
of 11,645 sq. miles. The remainder of the country totalling some 213,315
sq. miles comprises the Non-Scheduled Areas" (Ministry of Agriculture . . .,
1962: 3, footnote 3).

Like the Wakikuyu, the Wataita also practised the custom of clitoridectomy, but they responded differently. One explanation could be that the missionary sects in Taita did not feel as strongly as their counterparts in Ukikuyu on this issue.[3]

Christianity spread rapidly in Taita, especially after the turn of the century. The Gospels according to Saints Mark, John and Luke had already been translated into Kiswahili by 1904, 1905 and 1908 respectively. By 1922, the whole New Testament had been translated into Kitaita and had a second reprint in 1932 (Madoka, 1950: 15-16).

Whereby previous differentiation had been based on age and sex, Christian education and teaching became an independent differentiating variable in Taita and other African societies. In Taita, those who became Christians were known as *Washomi*, and those who did not were known as *Watasi*.[4] It was a section of the Washomi who founded the Taita Hills Association (THA) in 1938 to fight against the threat of further land alienation.[5] It was regarded as subversive and was proscribed in 1940 because of the 1939-1945 war (Bennett, 1963: 92-110).

The New Mood

European farming emerged from the war strengthened and more competitive. This was due in part to mechanization, the colonial government having used part of its share of the credit facilities provided to Great Britain by the United States during the war to purchase farm machinery. The Kenyan Government also provided settler farmers with credit facilities. In addition it offered these farmers fixed prices for bulk purchases of their crops, thus ensuring them sales and profits. Hence the war-time period gave the colonial régime the opportunity to entrench large-scale farming by providing financial backing, improving technical efficiency and intensifying its infrastructure (Van Zwanenberg, 1975: 201-226; Leys, 1975: 63-117). It is not surprising therefore that "under these circumstances it was inevitable that sooner or later European agriculture would show itself to be superior" (Van Zwanenberg, 1975: 45). It was on the European model that subsequent African agricultural development was to be based.

It was from their new vantage position that the settlers were able to back their mentor, the colonial régime, in launching a Ten Year Development Programme, 1946-1955, under the auspices of ALDEV. ALDEV's much acclaimed

---

[3]The dominant Christian sect in Taita is the Anglican Church Missionary Society (CMS) (see Chapter 3). The clitoridectomy controversy was started by the Church of Scotland Mission in Ukikuyu.

[4]*Washomi* literally means 'those who read', and *Watasi* 'those who worship'. Realizing that 'reading' is not holier than 'worshipping', the Anglicans referred to the non-Christians as *Wadawida* - i.e. Wataita - as if, on conversion to Christianity, a man ceased being a Mtaita! (Although culturally speaking, this perhaps is true.) The Roman Catholics decided to use Kiswahili or English words to refer to non-Christians: they are either *Washenzi* (primitives) or *Wapagani* (pagans).

[5]Similar associations had sprung up all over the country: Kikuyu Central Association (KCA) in 1925 (Thuku, 1970) and the Luo Thrift and Trading Corporation (Odinga, 1968: 79) are two of the most famous.

projects included Betterment Schemes, Rural Water Supplies, Animal Husbandry, Grazing Management, Agrarian Credit and Land Tenure Reform in African Lands. However, between 1946 and 1962 ALDEV was in fact to spend as little as 6 million pounds on the general improvement of African farming (Ministry of Agriculture, 1962).

With the European farming sector economically stronger, competition from 'progressive' African farmers became tolerable. For example, in 1946, 318 Africans were allowed to grow coffee.[6] Exposed to increasing socio-economic pressure, the system of communal land tenure started to disintegrate, especially in those areas where the pressure was heaviest. Clayton (1949) observed the following:

> "It is likely that this war-time experience, by changing the emphasis from subsistence to quasi-commercial agricultural economy, was one of the factors facilitating the general acceptance (in some areas at least) of subsequent reforms which aimed at the complete commercialization of agriculture."

Commercialization of agriculture was equivalent to land enclosure and consolidation,[7] in the case of the few emerging 'progressive' African farmers. The process had already been started by some farmers in Kipsigis as early as the late 1930s and 1940s, and by the early 1950s all the land had been enclosed. The Kipsigis farmers were followed by a similar enclosure movement in Kisii. In the 1950s the 'progressive' farmers of Elgeyo-Marakwet led a 'spontaneous' enclosure movement which involved the fencing of all the land in the higher Elgeyo Division. However, while the Government welcomed these developments, they were not officially recognized through registration or the issuing of title deeds (Verhelst, 1968: 438-439).

In Ukikuyu, where the combination of land shortage and the oppression of the colonial régime was more acutely felt than in any other part of the country, communal land tenure was rapidly being forced to give way to individualization of land rights, and already there was a growing demand for the issue and registration of land titles. Thus, by the late 1940s, voluntary consolidation among progressive farmers had started in North Tetu Division of Nyeri District under the leadership of Senior Chief Muhoya, a staunch loyalist. Using it for counter-insurgency purposes, the colonial régime took advantage of this 'spontaneous' process by rewarding the loyalists with individual

---

[6]It was also at this time that the participation of African 'progressives' in politics was beginning to be tolerated. Eliud Mathu was the first African to be nominated to the Legislative Council, in 1945.

[7]Historically, the terms *enclosure* and *consolidation* have almost the same meaning, both originating from the Enclosure Movement which took place in England between 1760 and 1860. It involved the aggregation of scattered fragments of land into one land holding which was fenced in; or fencing a holding by pushing out the people living on the land - as the settlers did when they alienated land from the Africans; or fencing communally owned land - as the 'progressives' were now doing. Verhelst (1968: 417) quotes Arthur Young, the chief apostle of the English Enclosure Movement, as saying "the magic of freehold turns sand to gold". However, Young was also to admit that "the poor are injured and most grossly".

title deeds after the outbreak of the Mau Mau peasant war in the early
1950s.[8]

The Administration's exploitation of tenurial change for counter-insurgency
purposes received an agronomic rationalization in 1954, after the publication
of the Swynnerton Plan. The Plan went a little further than merely supporting the Administration's manipulation of the tenurial change in the war-zone
areas. It advocated the expansion of this movement through the implementation of agrarian reform in the Non-Scheduled Areas. The Swynnerton Plan
was therefore made up of two complementary components: tenurial and agrarian
reforms. To facilitate its implementation, it divided African Lands into
four broad categories, which provide the basis of land classification right
up to the present day (see Table 5.1).

Table 5.1. Classification of Land in Non-Scheduled Areas*

Category of description	Characteristics	Area in sq. miles	Remarks
A – high potential; arable	25–35" rainfall; soil good	18,197	Includes all the arable land in Non-Scheduled Areas; suitable for intensive balanced mixed farming.
B – high potential; grazing	25–35" rainfall; soil mainly shallow; fertility and drainage problems	10,293	Cultivation would require costly maintenance of irrigation systems, swamp reclamation and flood control. Even now, farming in this area is discouraged by the Ministry of Agriculture.
C – low potential; grazing	20–25" rainfall; bush and tsetse-fly country	14,340	Suitable for stock grazing, horticultural development and afforestation – in conjunction with tetse reclamation.
D – very low potential; grazing	10–20" or less of erratic rainfall	147,884	Most suitable for (nomadic) pastoralism; and for wild animals.

*Based on The Swynnerton Plan, 1954 and the Ministry of Agriculture's
classifications of 1962.

[8]The loyalists, led by Senior Chief Muhoya, denounced the war at a huge rally
by saying, "Mau Mau has spoiled the country. Let Mau Mau perish for ever.
All people should search for Mau Mau and kill it" (Murray-Brown, 1972: 249).
The Chief was killed by the freedom fighters a few days later. Jomo
Kenyatta, who was also at this meeting, was arrested on 20 October 1950,
and a state of emergency was declared. See the following for an account of
the Mau Mau war: Kariuki, 1963; Barnett and Njama, 1966; Itote, 1967.

For the successful exploitation of the four major land categories, the Plan envisaged structural changes which were to involve "suitable reforms to the system of African customary land tenure and inheritance". African land-tenure systems, which were predominantly communal in nature, were to be 'reformed' to a freehold individual tenure system. As a market commodity, land could be bought and sold and, in addition, could act as security "against loans from Government or other approved agency". The individualization of both use and disposal rights was considered to be the cornerstone of agricultural development, because it created the appropriate environment necessary before a farmer could be encouraged to "invest his labour and profits into the development of his farm".

The structural changes to be brought about by tenurial reform were to be supported by the second dimension of land reform, namely, agrarian reform. The agrarian dimension demanded the modification of previous policies and the creation of a wide range of new conditions. The programme included the lifting of restrictions which prohibited African farmers from growing high-priced cash crops such as coffee and pyrethrum, and the rearing of exotic livestock. Credit facilities were expanded to include African farmers who possessed the necessary security (title deed).

Market facilities were provided at both district and provincial levels to give the farmer secure and profitable outlets for his produce. Similarly, technical inputs in the form of surveying, farm planning and agricultural field staff such as extension workers were proposed, together with the establishment of district land development boards and co-operative societies. Finally, there was a strong emphasis on agriculture in the education of farmers' children.

The Plan was to be implemented immediately in the high potential areas which included the following districts: North, Central and South Nyanza, Kericho, Nandi, Elgeyo cum West Säk, Nyeri, Fort Hall (Murang'a), Kiambu and Taita Hills.

The Swynnerton Plan got a further boost when the East African Royal Commission 1953-1955 recommended among other things "the breaking down of tribal and racial boundaries, and to replace them by confirming individual titles to land where they exist and to encourage their acquisition where they do not" (Report 56: Cmnd 9475).

Hence by the mid-1950s the claims concerning the unproductive nature of the traditional African land tenure systems seem to have been validated. Thus their reform was regarded as a prerequisite to sound agricultural development. What now remained to be done was the introduction of the appropriate legislative tools. In this context Okoth-Ogendo (1976: 164-167) notes the three-fold nature of this legislation, namely the Native Land Tenure Rules 1956, the Native Lands Registration Ordinance 1959, and the 1968 Land Acts.

Native Land Tenure Rules 1956 were promulgated to offer a legal cover (retrospectively in some respects) to the land-tenure changes which were already taking place 'spontaneously' in certain parts of the country. However, the Rules emphasized in S.68 that customary rights and interests were to be maintained:

"In respect of the occupation, use, control, inheritance, succession and
disposal of any land suitable in the Native Lands, every African tribe,
group, family and individual shall have all the rights which they enjoy
or may enjoy by virtue of existing native law and custom. . . ."

The Rules also laid down the process of tenure reform, which was to consist
of three stages: adjudication, consolidation and registration.

Adjudication is the ascertainment and recording of individual or group rights
and interests claimed over plots of land within a given area. These claims
were to be made to statutory boards - a Land Adjudication Committee and an
Arbitration Board. It was left to the relevant minister to declare an area
for adjudication if he was satisfied that existing private landholding in
the area that warranted such an action. This ministerial initiative was
qualified in the 1959 Ordinance, which required the minister to take such
action only "at the request of the local authorities". But the 1968
Adjudication Act restored ministerial initiative while maintaining the
provision for local authorities to submit their requests if they wished to
do so. Since land reform became national policy in 1968, the provision for
local authorities to request adjudication is no longer considered necessary.

Consolidation is the aggregation of sub-economic and/or excessively dispersed
and fragmented land plots into one landholding suitable for rational economic
exploitation. If by 'fragmentation' we mean "a stage in the evolution of an
agricultural holding in which a single farm consists of a number of separate
parcels of land often scattered over a wide area" (*JAA*, 1956: paras 48 and
49), then consolidation does help remedy the problem of fragmentation, but
not that of sub-division. The same source defines 'sub-division' as "a
process whereby a holding operated by one farmer is split into a number of
holdings operated by different farmers". It is a fact that customary
inheritance laws encourage the process of fragmentation. Hence, although
consolidation helps to eradicate fragmentation, it nevertheless fails to
arrest the process of sub-division.

Registration does not automatically follow consolidation; but "what better
than registration of title with all the advantages of registered
conveyancing?" (Verhelst, 1968: 418). The main function of the registration
of title is to enable the State to know relevant particulars, such as who
owns which farm holdings. But registration of title is not a magical
ingredient which will automatically lead to economic development. Indeed, it
is not essential at all, although a title deed is useful as a security.

Native Lands Registration Ordinance 1959 legalized individual freehold land
tenure. Under S.37(a) any person could have a freehold title to land vested
in him, provided that he was registered as the proprietor. Having done so,
he could then enjoy "all rights and privileges belonging or appurtenant
thereto . . ." His rights and privileges were protected under S.89(1), which
declared that first registration was unchallengeable in a court of law, even
if it was fraudulently obtained. Another implication of this provision was
that registration meant an automatic annulment of existing communal rights
and interests under the communal land tenure system. Thus the anomaly
contained in S.68 of the 1956 Rules was removed.

Together with the registration statute was the Land Control Ordinance (Native
Lands) which was instrumental to the establishment of Provincial and District
Land Control Boards. The main purpose of these boards was to control land
transactions and to make sure that the functioning of the land market -
itself an offshoot of the registration statute - would not encourage the

phenomenon of landlessness. If Land Control Boards were meant to control land transactions within an environment in which a free land market was simultaneously being established and legalized, then a conflict between the two statutes (both in the same ordinance) seemed inevitable.

1968 Land Acts: Consolidation, Adjudication, Group Representative: By 1968 the original 1959 Ordinance had been modified by various amendments and repeals but was still managing to maintain its fundamentals. The Ordinance had been renamed the Land Adjudication Act, only to be renamed again in 1968 as the Land Consolidation Act when a new adjudication statute, the Land Adjudication Statute, was passed to deal with "those areas in which the process of consolidation is not appropriate. The only significant addition . . . is that it provides for the adjudication of group rights and interests as well as individual interests" (Okoth-Ogendo, 1976: 167). This provision made it possible for pastoralists to operate group ranching through their co-ownership of a common title to land. The Group Represent- ative Statute was the enabling Act.

The success of the thesis which argued that communal tenure was an outmoded institution holding up the 'modernization' of African agriculture, had its concrete manifestation in the number of Land Acts passed between 1956 and 1968, which facilitated the establishment of a tenure system based on individual freehold title. Land reform was introduced in Taita in 1969 under the terms contained in the 1959 Ordinance. Part Three of this book is devoted to an examination and analysis of the events brought about by the interrelationships between the exogenous variables, land reform and formal education, and the internal ones, population growth and rural poverty.

PART THREE

Population Growth and Socio-economic Changes

CHAPTER 6

Population Growth and Demographic Pressure in Taita: Migration as a Response

Historical Background

The exact population of Taita was unknown until 1948, the year of the first general census for the whole country. Prior to this, estimates of the size of Kenya's population - as well as of Taita's population - were arrived at by two methods. The first was simple guesswork, used by the early European adventurers and colonial administrators. Thus Kenya's population was guessed to be anything from 450,000 to 2½ million in 1897, and about 4 million in 1902 (Van Zwanenberg, 1975: 7). The second method of estimating population size was by using recorded information such as Poll and Hut tax returns or records kept by missionaries. The Kenya Land Commission of 1932-1934 relied on such data for their estimates.

Whatever the method, it is now generally agreed that the population of Kenya - and by inference, Taita - declined during the first two decades of this century (see Chapter 4). Its upward trend started around the mid-1920s, using as an indicator a study of 698 Taita families made during an 11-year period from 1920 to 1931. The data, collected by the Bura Catholic Mission and later analysed by Kuczynski, gives the annual figures of births, infant mortality and children dying under 1 year of age (see Table 6.1). The phenomenon of a sharp drop in the infant mortality rate is well illustrated in graph form (see Graph 6.1).

Table 6.1. Annual Figures of Births, Infant Mortality and Deaths under 1 Year of 698 Taita Families, 1920-1931[*]

Year	1920	1921	1922	1923	1924	1925	1926	1927	1928	1929	1930	1931
Births	72	83	69	95	99	92	112	119	114	134	93	64
Deaths under 1 yr	6	8	22	20	32	22	14	11	15	19	11	12
Infant mortality	83	96	174	210	323	240	125	92	131	142	118	188

[*]Source: R. R. Kuczynski, 1949: 150.

69

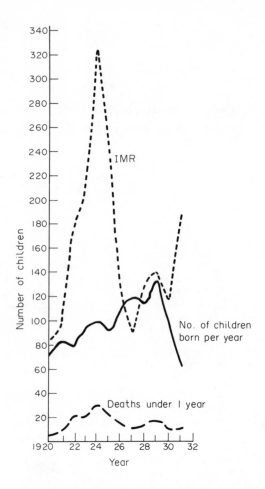

Graph 6.1. Birth and Infant Mortality Rate of 698 Taita
Families 1920-1931.

In the early 1930s the population of Taita was estimated to be about 39,674
(KLC Report, 1933: 319), while in 1938 it was about 37,471 (Kuczynski,
1949: 150). In the 1948 general census the District was found to have
62,051 people. Prior to the census, it had been estimated that children
formed about 37 percent of the total population, but the 1948 census showed
that in fact children made up 48 percent of the entire population. It is
now generally concluded that "all the earlier estimates were too low by
25 percent or possibly more" (Van Zwanenberg, 1975: 8). The reason for such
an error was the underestimation of the adult/child ratio.

There was a second general census in 1962, when the District's population was found to be 89,356 (*Kenya Population Census 1962*, Vol.III: 20). This gives an inter-censal increase of 44 percent. The total annual fertility rate for the whole country was 6.8 children per woman within child-bearing age, while there was a crude annual birth rate of 48-51 per thousand (*Kenya Population Census 1962*, Vol.III: 69). The crude annual death rate was between 18-25 per thousand, and expectation of life at birth was estimated to be 39 years (*ibid*: 77). In specifying the natural rate of increase, it was felt prudent to hold to a 1960 estimate, which located it within the narrower range of 27 and 31 per thousand, rather than by the 1962 figures, which estimated a wider range of 23 and 33 per thousand. Thus, relying on the 1960 figures, the natural rate of increase was calculated to be between 2.7 and 3.1 percent per annum (*ibid*.: 77).

In 1969 the District's population was 110,742 (*Kenya Population Census 1969*, Vol.I: 21-22). This registers a natural rate of increase of 3.4 percent per annum.[1] The female population made up 51 percent of the total and the sex ratio stood at 97 - in other words, for every 100 women, there were 97 men.

The 'ethnic' composition of the population was as follows: 91,732 (83 percent) Wataita,[2] 7289 (7 percent) Wataveta (*ibid*.) and 11,721 (10 percent) 'outsiders' - i.e. those from outside the District. Assuming that each of these ethnic groups has been maintaining a uniform rate of increase of 3.4 percent per annum, the estimated population of the District should have been in the region of 140,000 by the end of 1977.[3] In this case the ethnic composition of the population would be as shown in Table 6.2.

Table 6.2. Projection of the District's Population Size by the End of 1977

Ethnic group	Number	Percentage
(a) Wataita	116,000	83
(b) Wataveta	9,800	7
(c) Others	14,200	100
Total	140,000	100

---

[1]World Bank *Atlas* (1976: 4) gives this rate as the national rate of growth. The same source gives the national rate of growth as 3.6 percent per annum in its 1975 edition.

[2]Wasagalla and Wakasigau are regarded as Wataita in national census data.

[3]In 1973, the Taita-Taveta *Annual Report* (1976: 1) estimated the District's population to be 120,000 people. It was estimated to be 128,379 by 1975 (see footnote 7 on p.19).

The Demography of a Taita Micro-Society

The micro-study among the Taita, which forms an integral part of this study, supported the macro-analysis in terms of rapidly increasing rates of population growth.[4] The total population of the micro-society is 2592, made up of 1235 (48 percent) males and 1357 (52 percent) females. The age distribution and sex ratio is shown in Table 6.3.[5]

Table 6.3.   Taita Age Distribution and Sex Ratio

Age group	Male		Female		S.R.
	No.	%	No.	%	
0-4	204	16.52	239	17.62	85
5-10	371	30.04	394	29.03	94
15-44	498	40.32	569	41.93	88
45+	162	13.12	155	11.42	105
Total	1235	100.00	1357	100.00	91

Fertility is indicated by the mean parity ratio of women between 40-49 years of age, which is 7.94. This means that on average a woman has a total number of eight live births within her fertility cycle. But the mean number of live births born to all women aged between 15-49 is 4.05, with a crude birth rate (CBR) of 50.95 per thousand population.

Mortality is shown by the proportion of live births now dead for women aged between 15-49, which is 0.147. The crude death rate (CDR) is 13.95 per thousand population, with a life expectation at birth of 51 and 49 for females and males respectively, averaging at 50 years for both sexes.

While 4.05 is the mean number of live births for women aged between 15-49, the mean number of live births surviving per woman is 3.45. With a CBR of 50.95 per thousand and a CDR of 13.93 per thousand, the crude rate of natural increase comes to 3.70 percent per annum. This is higher than the 1962-1969 inter-censal rate of increase of 3.4 percent. Indeed, while 3.7 percent should be regarded as a crude rate of population growth, it still goes to show how fast the population is increasing – definitely at a rate of not less than 3.5 percent, which is still very high.

Man-Land Ratio: The relationship between man and land becomes more signifi-cant in such a situation of rapid population growth, especially when land is the population's major resource. The increase in population density between 1948 and 1977 is shown in Table 6.4.

---

[4]The demographic indices have been computed from the raw population data collected in the field with the help of the Project's demographic consultant, Tim Dyson.

[5]For age distribution according to age cohorts, see Population Pyramid, Appendix III.

Table 6.4. Taita-Taveta Population Density, 1948-1977

Year	Land area in sq. miles	Density per sq. mile	Source
1948	6013	6	Kuczynski, 1949, Vol.II: 150
1962	5899	15	*Kenya Census 1962*, Vol.III: 20, Table III: 2
1969	6722*	16	*Kenya Census 1969*, Vol.I: 21
1977	6625**	21	Author's measurement

*17,209 sq.km converted into sq. miles.
**16,959 sq.km from *Statistical Abstract*, 1975: 13, Table 13, converted into sq. miles.

Two things can be immediately deduced from the density figures. Firstly, population density has more than tripled within a 30-year period, providing yet another indicator of a rapidly growing population. Secondly, while the population is growing rapidly, even at this rate the density will only be 62 per square mile in 30 years time. Such a figure might not appear so alarming on paper.

However, population-density figures fail to reflect the geographical distribution of the population, which is largely determined by the carrying capacity of the land. Dealing with the Taita part of the District, one finds that population is mainly concentrated in the Taita Hills proper, Sagalla and Kasigau. These three areas coincide with the three 'ethnic' groups which are commonly referred to as Wataita. According to the *Kenya Census 1969* (Vol.III: 71), the District's indigenous population was 99,021, i.e. 90 percent of the entire population. This figure is the sum total of 91,732 Wataita and 7289 Wataveta. The 'ethnic' composition of this indigenous population, according to the 1969 figures, is shown in Table 6.5. I have divided the 'Wataita' into its three components and calculated the population size for each group from the figures found in the *Kenya Census 1969* (Vol.I: 21-22).

Table 6.5. Ethnic Composition of the Indigenous Population of Taita-Taveta District

Ethnic group	Number	Percentage
Wataita proper	79,966	81
Wasagalla	7703	8
Wakasigau	4063	4
Wataveta	7289	7
Total	99,021	100

The heaviest population concentration is found in the Taita Hills, the 'homeland' of 72 percent of the District's entire population. The total area of the Taita Hills is just about 300 square miles, thus giving a population density of 267 people per square mile. However, as I have already pointed

out (see p.84), only 42.5 percent of the total land area in the Taita Hills
is cultivatable - i.e. 128 square miles. In 1969 the population density on
cultivatable land was 625 per square mile. Such a figure gives a more
relevant and accurate picture of the man/land ratio than those given in
Table 6.4. Table 6.6 further highlights the phenomenon of the man/land ratio
in Taita given annual population increases of 3.5 percent.

Table 6.6. Population Density in the Taita Hills

Year	Per sq. mile of total land area	Per sq. mile of cultivatable land
1969	267	625
1977	339	795

The Response to Demographic Pressure: Since the 1920s the rapid growth in
population, in conjunction with external factors such as the establishment of
the native reserves, has exacerbated the socio-economic conditions in the
Taita Hills. The early response to the population pressure was to populate
the lowlands and also the practice of a transhumance type of agriculture
between the high and low zones. When these measures were dislocated by the
intrusion of colonialism, the Hills were more intensively exploited, leading
to long-term land wastage in the form of soil erosion and exhaustion.

One attempt to resolve the problems generated by demographic pressure was
made by the colonial régime in the early 1950s, when it established a
settlement scheme in the Shimba Hills in Kwale District, just south of
Mombasa. The settlement was originally earmarked to cater for the excess
Taita population. Instead the scheme attracted the Wakamba rather than the
Wataita (Ministry of Agriculture, 1962: 201). One of the reasons for the
recalcitrance of the Wataita was their mistrust of the colonial régime. They
thought they were being tricked so that their land could be made available to
white settlers. It was a fear based on concrete evidence, for it should not
be forgotten that there was a white man's coffee farm in Wundanyi, the
heartland of Taita. Furthermore, the Government was carving out large tracts
of land from the surrounding lower zone for the sisal estates in Voi,
Mwatate and Kedai. This was further proof which sustained the fears of the
Wataita and discouraged them from migrating.

As might be expected, the colonial government explained the Wataita's lack
of co-operation in terms of either their conservatism (including their
reluctance to leave their ancestral graves), or their lack of enterprise.
Even today, the Government sometimes has similar attitudes, as for example
expressed in the much bandied-about jokes about the coast people sitting
under coconut trees waiting for the coconuts to fall, or their being
concerned with witchcraft. Such attitudes are taken up when it is necessary
to justify the 'tribally-biased' implementation of national policies.

But such explanations are not borne out in reality at the grassroots level.
That people are motivated to migrate to less densely populated areas in order
to reduce demographic pressures is no less true of the Wataita than anyone
else. Hence, while they would not migrate to the Shimba Hills, they have

migrated to Taveta and are still doing so.[6]

The extent of migration by the Wataita to other parts of the country is
illustrated by the 1969 Census figures, which recorded 33 percent of the
entire population not resident in the District. Seven years earlier non-
residents formed only 14 percent of the population. The resident and non-
resident Taita population is summarized in Table 6.7.

Table 6.7. 1969 Resident and Non-resident Taita Population

	Numbers		Percentages	
Resident in district		61,769		67
Non-resident:				
elsewhere in Province	19,112		21.0	
elsewhere in Kenya	6878	29,963	8.0	33
outside Kenya	478		0.5	
not stated	3495		3.5	
Total		91,732		100.0

Based on the *Kenya Census* figures (*1969*, Vol.III: 71).

Thus, by 1969, 64 percent of the non-resident Taita population (21 percent
of the total) were resident elsewhere in the Coast Province. Of these,
76 percent (14,553) resided in Mombasa (*Kenya Census 1969*, Vol.II: 4,
Table 3). Of non-residents who lived outside the Province (but within Kenya),
46 percent lived in Nairobi (3185). Thus 19 percent of the total Taita
population resided in either Mombasa or Nairobi, most of them in Mombasa. If
other urban centres such as Nakuru, Kisumu, Thika and Eldoret are taken into
consideration, then by 1969 the Taita 'urban population' made up over 20 percent of the entire Wataita.

The extent of Taita migration to urban areas stands out when compared to
another Kenyan society, for instance the Mijikenda, who occupy two districts
of the Coast Province - namely, Kilifi and Kwale. According to the *Kenya
Census* (*1969*, Vol.III: 71), their total population was over half a million,
thus outnumbering the Wataita by six to one. Table 6.8 indicates the
propensity to migrate among the Wataita in relative terms.

---

[6]My attempts to collect census data for Taita's migrants to Taveta were
frustrated. However, their numerical superiority is illustrated by the fact
that the immediate Former Taveta member of Parliament was a Mtaita.

Table 6.8. Populations of the Wataita and Wamijikenda,
based on the Kenya Census, 1969

| | Percentages of urban population[*] | | Total |
	Mombasa	Nairobi	
Wataita	82	18	100
Wamijikenda	97	3	100

[*]Urban population here refers only to Mombasa and
Nairobi, migration to smaller urban centres being of
minor significance.

The Mijikenda urban population is concentrated in Mombasa, the town being
located within their territory. While the Wataita in Mombasa are fewer in
number, they are generally better educated and therefore better off in terms
of income-earning capacity. In 1969 the Wataita as a whole had a literacy
rate of 31 percent as compared to the Wamijikenda's 11 percent.[7] The
difference is well demonstrated by the fact that in Nairobi, Wataita
outnumber Wamijikenda by six to one.

Rural to urban migration is the outcome of three factors. First there is the
'push' factor in the form of demographic and other forces. Second, the urban
centres constitute the 'pull' factor, epitomized by the 'bright lights'
theory. The intermediary between these two factors is the 'literacy' factor.
The higher the literacy of the migrant,[8] the more favourable the conditions
for the pull factor to operate and the push factor to be effective.

Where the Mijikenda and Wataita are concerned, the influence of the push
factor due to demographic pressure is less effective in Kilifi and Kwale
than in Taita. In addition, with its higher literacy rate, the demographic
conditions prevailing in Taita cause the Wataita to become more responsive to
the pull factors than the Wamijikenda. This explains why, when compared
with the Wamijikenda, the propensity of the Wataita to migrate to Nairobi
stands out - Nairobi being relatively distant for both societies.

The rural to urban migrant does not in fact regard himself as a migrant,
since he is still tied to his economic assets and family back in the rural
area, where he expects to return.[9] His problem therefore is not to reproduce
his economic assets in his urban environment, but rather to earn enough so
that he can remit more to improve and expand his assets 'back home'. His
ability to create for himself an urban home as well depends on the
remunerativeness of his job, which depends on his qualifications. Hence,

---

[7]The national literacy rate is 27 percent. I have calculated these literacy
percentages from the 1969 Census figures, Vol.III.

[8]This should be considered in relative terms, because of the economic bias
inherent in the push factor and the tendency therefore to keep re-defining
qualificatory standards as unemployment rises (see Dore, 1976).

[9]The wages offered him in the urban centres clearly reinforce this (see
footnote 1/87).

his qualifications determine the type of employment he gets, which in turn
determines his urban socialization, which may be roughly at one of three
socio-economic levels, namely: lumpenproletariat, proletariat or bourgeois.[10]
The migrant's income in turn determines his ability to invest in his rural
home.

Up to this point, I have identified migration as one major response to
demographic pressure. Further, I have noted that it has two main permutations, rural to urban migration and rural to rural (intra-rural) migration.
Intra-rural migration takes place in two ways. Firstly, it takes the form
of pre-planned settlement programmes undertaken by the Government in response
to demographic pressure. As far as Kenya is concerned, it is doubtful
whether settlement schemes are in fact solving the problems generated by
demographic pressure; rather, they are exacerbating the political situation
arising out of such schemes (Wassermen, 1973). Secondly, intra-rural
migration takes the form of spontaneous and uncoordinated movements to new
areas of settlement, when peasants themselves take the initiative. Whatever
the disadvantages of intra-rural migration (if any), in the long run it does
seem to contribute to a decrease of demographic pressure, in that it is a
measure undertaken on a permanent basis. But with land being a finite
resource, this type of response should be regarded as an intermediary step.
Unless there is a marked decline in population growth and/or rapid economic
growth to provide employment opportunities, acute discontentment is bound to
arise.

Unlike the migrant to the city, the intra-rural migrant, with very few
exceptions, literally transplants his household into a new environment. In
so doing he forfeits his assets in his old home and tries to reproduce and
expand them in his new home. The decision to migrate, in contrast to the
rural to urban migrant, is not usually taken under external enticement, but
rather from the individual's personal awareness, motivation and interests.[11]

At the same time, the intra-rural migrant usually wishes to maintain his
kinship ties with his old home, although this is not necessarily true where
his offspring are concerned. There are bound to be attitudinal changes
towards the ancestral home as time goes by. How fast these changes take place
depends on the pioneer migrant's success in his new home. What appears to be
most often the case is that the poorer migrants maintain regular contact with
their relatives back home, the richer and more successful migrants less so.

A case at hand here is Family K. The elder K migrated permanently with his
three wives from Shigaro, Taita, to Kimorigo in Taveta in 1953. He was a
pioneer in the cultivation of cotton and cereal production using irrigation.
He invested the money he earned by sending his children to school. As his
children grew up and gained salaried employment in towns, he deftly managed
the cash remunerations he received from them. At the same time, skilful
management of his household labour resources (he hired casual labour at peak
periods) enabled him to further expand and invest both in farming and in
the education of his younger children. The success of his brand of household

---

[10] In explaining 'tribal' conglomerates in urban or semi-urban areas, more
often than not it is the inhabitants' tribal identities rather than their
socio-economic status which have been emphasized (see Parkin, 1969).

[11] In a few instances, migration to Taveta offers Taita's social deviants
(such as incestuous sinners) a sanctuary where they can rebuild their
lives.

management stands out clearly when one looks at the educational achievements
of his children: eight (three of them daughters) are university graduates.
As he became more prosperous, the elder K came to depend less on kinship tie
in Taita.   As for his children and grandchildren, they have come to identify
themselves more with Taveta than with Taita.   When a member of this family
meets one of his poorer relatives from Taita, it tends to be the latter who
actively seeks to establish a close kin relationship.

Migration being a spontaneous response to demographic pressure by the
peasants, the Government also has been attempting to tackle the problems of
demographic pressure through its settlement schemes, within the context of
its land-reform programme.   The Government's commitment to implement land
reform, which is aimed at the individualization of land tenure, rests on the
assumptions that land is better managed when owned individually, is a suitable security for loans from the Government, banks or load-giving agencies
and finally that the process of individualization involves the redistribution of land.

The following chapter attempts to situate the implementation of land reform
and its ramifications within a socio-economic environment at the grassroots
level.

CHAPTER 7

Average Landholding and Land Distribution

The Average Holding

It was believed by the authorities that the success or failure of land reform rested on the formulation of a programme adaptable enough to eliminate the contradiction bound to arise by the interaction of the two main variables - population and land, with land being a finite resource.

Right from the time when the idea of carrying out land reform was first mooted, the reformers have had to contend with the problem of defining the size of the minimum or 'average' holding necessary for the 'average' household's survival. The average holding had to satisfy two important functional requirements.

First, the holding should be of a size capable of allowing its household to produce a surplus. According to Swynnerton, the average holding should have the potential of raising the household's surplus "from a few pounds a year to something of the order of £100 a year" (1954: 58).

The second requirement was that the holding should have the capacity to accommodate the household's population increase through natural growth.

In the 1930s, it was estimated that the average Taita household of 4.6 people needed a 40-acre holding to meet its basic minimum requirements (KLC *Evidence*, 1934, Vol.III: 2734).[1] The actual cultivatable land available per household then was on average 6.19 acres (KLC *Evidence*, 1934, Vol.III: 2793).

Humphrey estimated the utilization of the average holding in South Nyeri (Central Province) in the mid-1940s to be no more than 6.5 acres (see Table 7.1).

---

[1] The Commission did not state whether this holding was for shifting or permanent cultivation.

Table 7.1. Envisaged Land Utilization on an Average
            Holding, Early 1940s[*]

		Acres
(i)	Under crops	2.80
(ii)	Fallow	0.55
(iii)	House, etc.	0.50
	Total:	3.85
(iv)	Balance, including forests, rough grazing, etc.	2.65
	Total:	6.50

[*]Source: Humphrey, 1945: 52.

By the late 1940s, experimentation at Bukura Agricultural School led to the proposition that 12 acres was the 'ideal' economic size for a holding. In fact, the School's calculations showed that the ideal economic holding would consist of 6 acres; *but*, taking into account the natives' inability to cultivate intensively mixed farming on such a plot of land, it was considered necessary to add an extra 6 acres to take care of their extensive cultivation practices. In addition, the extra acres were intended to cater for the household's total needs (see Table 7.2).

Table 7.2. Envisaged Land Utilization on an Average
            Holding, Late 1940s[*]

		Acres
(i)	Cultivation (already planted)	3.00
(ii)	Temporary ley " "	3.00
(iii)	Timber plot " "	0.75
(iv)	House, vegetable garden and compound (prepared)	0.25
(v)	Permanent pasture (preparing)	5.00
	Total:	12.00

[*]Source: Humphrey 1945: 68.

Swynnerton did not give a specific acreage to qualify his notion of holdings "of a size economic for the purpose for which they are required" in his plan (1954: 8). He did not do so because, unlike the previous land-tenure reformers, he was not considering the native population in its entirety, but rather, since land was an exhaustible commodity, a lucky minority. Consequently, he held the population variable relatively constant, estimatin; the beneficiaries of his reform programme to be about 600,000 households, and limiting these to the high potential area. He was interested in allowin; the 'market' forces to operate freely, even at the cost of creating a land-less class, for he argued that such an outcome was a normal and necessary

step in the evolution of a country (1954: 10).[2] If one is to take the total
acreage of 11,646,080 in the high potential area, allocated to 600,000 households, then it can perhaps be assumed that his notion of a holding of
economic size was somewhere between 15 and 20 acres (1954: 10-29).

In Central Province, the minimum size farm was not to be less than 7.5 acres,
which was considered to be a size economically viable for cash-cropping. Yet
after the implementation of land reform, 86 percent of all registered holdings were less than the statutory 7.5 acres (Van Zwanenberg, 1975: 53). By
1968, out of 43,200 registered holdings in Nyeri District, 34,500 (80 percent)
were of 6 acres or less (Verhelst, 1968: 419).

Whatever the farm size - and it seems to be generally agreed that 6 acres is
the theoretical minimum - its consolidation and registration does not
guarantee its sanctity. For fragmentation sets in at random through sub-
division, either according to customary law of inheritance or on a willing-
seller willing-buyer basis. Hence, for example, by 1970 registered land
holdings in Kiambu District (Central Province) were as follows:

    20 percent under 1 acre;
    35 percent under 2 acres;
    77 percent under 6 acres (Van Zwanenberg, 1975: 53).

Land Distribution

Working on the premise that the Government is committed to a "more equitable
distribution of resources and income",[3] land reform may be regarded as one of
the tools available for achieving this goal. Land reform aims at the fulfilment of two interrelated functions: firstly, to provide an average holding
of economic size whose potential enables a household to generate a surplus;
and secondly, to act as a leveller in the distribution of resources and
income. At this point, I turn to my case-study sample to examine the extent
to which land reform meets its goals at the grassroots level.

The sub-location of Shigaro-Sungululu has 1050 registered holdings, totalling
1800 acres.[4] This gives an average holding of 1.7 acres. The biggest holding is 13.6 acres, while the smallest is 0.1 acre. Certainly, an average of
1.7 acres per household hardly compares favourably with the niggardly pre-
independence estimation of 6 acres as the basic minimum for an average holding. However, the Shigaro-Sungululu figure does not tell the whole story
since it does not show how the land is distributed *within* a household. In
other words, what is the *per capita* distribution of an average holding of
1.7 acres?[5]

---

[2]These same sentiments are echoed over 20 years later by Holtham and
Hazlewood (1976: 25), when they say that "greater inequality may be accompanied by, *and indeed be a condition of*, a general rise in living standards"
(author's emphasis).

[3]His Excellency the President Mzee Jomo Kenyatta, in his introduction to the
1974/78 *Development Plan*.

[4]See *Survey of Kenya*, Nairobi, 1970 Registry Index Maps, Orig. Nos. K 263,
264, 286, 287, 288, 309, 310, 311, 333, 356 and 357.

[5]To calculate the *per capita* distribution I divided a holding's acreage by
the *de jure* members of the household living off that land.

To examine the dynamics of land distribution and demographic forces at micro
level, I decided to work with a core sample of sixteen households. But
first, the 'household' within the Taita context needs to be defined. A
household is a combination of three analytically separable units. Firstly,
as a social unit which includes an individual living by himself/herself, a
nuclear family or an extended family.[6] Secondly, as a residential unit,
which is the same as the social unit with the exception that the separate
nuclear families which make up an extended family regard themselves as
individual economic units although they share the same residential compound.
Thirdly, as an economic unit, which to all intents and purposes is the
nuclear family both at the social and residential levels, but tied to a
larger group in regard to land rights, use and ownership.[7]

Taking indices such as size of holding, income and my subjective in-depth
knowledge of the sixteen households as criteria for categorization, I
divided the sample into four strata with four households making up each
stratum. The strata are graded from One (the poorest) to Four (the richest)
(see Table 7.3).

Table 7.3. Household and Holding Size per Stratum

Stratum One			Stratum Two		
Name	Household size	Acres	Name	Household size	Acres
Kirigha	6	1.2	Shako	3	5.2
Kiongo	13	4.3	Ngali	8	3.0
Kalaghe	7	1.5	Mwangemi	10	0.6
Mwakio	11	1.0	Mwanyama	7	2.0
Total	37	8.0	Total	28	10.0
Average	9.2	2.0	Average	7.0	2.7
Stratum Three			Stratum Four		
Name	Household size	Acres	Name	Household size	Acres
Kinyavura	15	3.1	Mwachugha	5	8.4
Mnjama	9	6.7	Mwazera	11	4.0
Mwandondo	9	6.1	Mwawuganga	3	7.3
Mlolwa	8	5.0	Mugho	7	10.3
Total	41	20.9	Total	26	30.0
Average	10.2	5.2	Average	6.5	7.5

[6]The terms 'household' and 'family' are interchangeable in this text.

[7]This definition of a household is very close to that given in Ministry of
Finance and Planning, 1977: 19-20.

By collapsing the four strata into two the average distribution is 2.4 and
6.4 acres for the poor and rich strata respectively. (Henceforth, for want
of a better term, I call Strata One and Two the 'poor' and Three and Four
the 'rich' strata.) On the other hand, the dynamism of land distribution is
shown by *per capita* ownership on an intra-household as well as on an inter/
intra-strata basis, as shown in Table 7.4.

Table 7.4. Intra-household and Inter/Intra-strata Land
            Distribution

Stratum One			Stratum Two		
Name	Acres	*Per capita* acreage	Name	Acres	*Per capita* acreage
Kirigha	1.2	0.2	Shako	5.2	1.7
Kiongo	4.3	0.3	Ngali	3.0	0.4
Kalaghe	1.5	0.2	Mwangemi	0.6	0.06
Mwakio	1.0	0.09	Mwanyama	2.0	0.3
Per capita average:		0.2	Per capita average:		0.6

Stratum Three			Stratum Four		
Name	Acres	*Per capita* acreage	Name	Acres	*Per capita* acreage
Kinyavura	3.1	1.7	Mwachugha	8.4	1.7
Mnjama	6.7	0.7	Mwazera	4.0	0.4
Mwandondo	6.1	0.7	Mwawuganga	7.3	2.4
Mlolwa	5.0	0.6	Mugho	10.3	1.5
Per capita average:		0.6	Per capita acreage:		1.5

Intra-household land distribution clearly depicts economic differentiation
both at the inter and intra-strata levels. The manifestation of this
phenomenon at inter-strata level is illustrated by the size of the *per capita*
average holdings of the two extreme strata, One and Four. The poorest
stratum's *per capita* average holding is 0.2 acre while the richest is 1.5
acres. The average *per capita* holding among the poor is 0.4 acres and among
the rich 1.05 acres.

Skewed land distribution in favour of the rich strata is further pronounced
by calculating the *per capita* household average holding for male children
only (see Table 7.5).

Table 7.5.   Intra-household and Inter/Intra-strata Land
             Distribution for Male Children Only

Stratum One			Stratum Two		
Name	No. of male children	Per capita acreage	Name	No. of male children	Per capita acreage
Kirigha	4	0.3	Shako	-*	-
Kiongo	4	1.1	Ngali	2	1.5
Kalaghe	5	0.3	Mwangemi	-*	-
Mwakio	3	0.3	Mwanyama	4	0.5
Average	4.0	0.5	Average	1.5	.5

Stratum Three			Stratum Four		
Name	No. of male children	Per capita acreage	Name	No. of male children	Per capita acreage
Kinyavura	6	0.5	Mwachugha	1	8.4
Mnjama	2	3.4	Mwazera	4	1.0
Mwandondo	3	2.0	Mwawuganga	1	7.3
Mlolwa	4	1.3	Mugho	3	3.4
Average	3.7	1.8	Average	2.3	5.0

*No male children yet, and if the parents die without having a male child,
the land will be inherited by the husband's brothers or the patrilineal
male next of kin (see Chapter 2, pp.54-57).

The calculation of the average size of the per capita holding for male
children per stratum throws into relief the differentiation of land distribution at inter-strata level.

The average per capita holding for male children in the poor and rich strata
is 0.5 acre and 3.4 acres respectively.

The preceding argument distinguishes the maldistribution of land at two
levels of abstraction: intra- and inter-strata levels. What then is the
distinction between them?

The possession of unequal sized holdings by households found in the same
stratum is the archtypal manifestation of this type of land maldistribution.
Nevertheless, this should not be attributed to land reform per se. It must
be remembered here that land was maldistributed even in pre-reform days.
But the tenure system which existed then was endowed with mitigatory factors
which successfully hid the intra-strata level (and inter-strata) uneven land
distribution so well that it never became a mechanism of differentiation
(see p.55).

Among other things, land reform has unfrozen these mitigatory factors,
unleashing the potency which had so far been unable to turn the phenomenon of
unequal distribution of land into a differentiating variable.

Tenure reform has injected into a relatively dormant system at the intra-
level a coagulate which makes it easier to classify households according to
the size of land they possess. By so doing, this has helped to develop a
stratified society based on inter- and intra-strata (and even intra-household)
differentiation. At this level of differentiation, the process is accentuated by the fact that the individual household's exposure to 'external'
inputs (which form the fulcrum in maintaining and reproducing the inter-
strata differentiation) is determined by the socio-economic status of its
'host' stratum.[8] This is borne out by the fact that although 73 percent of
the sample's adult population come from the poor strata, the average *per
capita* holding to be inherited by their male children is a mere 14 percent
of the average *per capita* holding to be inherited by their counterparts from
the rich strata (see Table 7.5).

Whatever the unequal distribution of land, an average holding of 1.7 acres
in Taita is meagre, and one is driven to wonder how the smallest holdings
managed to become registered at all. It appears that before consolidation
no attempt was made to work out a minimum-sized holding for registration.
The absence of a statutory minimum has given free vent to the buying and
selling of land at the gathering stage[9] prior to consolidation. Moreover,
the practice of buying and selling has continued since consolidation -
though illegally in some cases - thus furthering fragmentation.

---

[8]A number of studies have shown that the more land and the higher the income
a household has, the more advice and credit it gets from the sources of
external inputs (see Leys, 1975: 101, footnote 99).

[9]The gathering stage is the period of assessment in preparation for
consolidation.

CHAPTER 8

Population as a Labour Resource

The Sample Population and its Composition

My sample of sixteen households has a total population of 132 people. Out of this total population, 44 percent is male and 56 percent is female. Children between 0-14 years make up 54 percent of the total, with the 0-4 age cohort contributing 18 percent and the remaining 36 percent made up by the 5-14 age cohort (see Table 8.1).

Table 8.1. Age Distribution and Sex Ratios in Sample Households

Age group	Males	Females	Sex ratio	
0-4	8 (14%)	16 (22%)	50	69
5-14	21 (36%)	26 (35%)	81	
15-44	24 (41%)	27 (36%)	89	90
45+	5 (9%)	5 (7%)	100	
Total	58 (100%)	74 (100%)		

Thus it is a young population, with 81 percent of its members under 20 years of age (see Appendix III).

A dependency ratio is of little relevance as far as this study is concerned because of the value-loaded nature of the mathematical formula used to compute the ratio. The formula assumes that persons between 0-14 and over 65 years of age are not working and therefore unproductive. Instead, they are 'dependent' on 'working' persons of ages 15-64. While this may be true in many industrialized societies where child labour is no longer required and where many people retire when they reach the age of 65, it is less true in many non-industrialized societies.

As far as the young and old in Taita are concerned, their dependence ought to be assessed by finding out at what age and to what extent they contribute to productive labour. My argument is that there exists an interdependence within a household between the so-called dependent and working persons which renders the computation of a dependency ratio using the present-day demographic formula less meaningful. In the following pages I analyze the distribution and utilization of labour both within the individual household and at the inter-household level, in order to highlight the role of children in the household economy.

Labour Utilization: With few exceptions, I found that the household provides its own source of labour; with the availability of labour at its disposal being determined more or less by the number of its members. Whatever the source or size of its labour supply, the most important factor is how a household utilizes it.

My sample utilizes its labour in sixteen major activities which I annotate below in order of frequency. The frequency that an activity is carried out is given in brackets. Frequency here is a combination of two factors: the number of times the activity is carried out; and the number of people who engage in this activity.[1]

Cooking (20.6 percent) includes any type of meal preparation, including
    the making of tea and coffee;
Water-fetching (10.9 percent) from a river or common tap for domestic use;
Shamba work (10.8 percent) of all types, such as cultivation, weeding,
    manuring, planting and harvesting.
School (10.6 percent) attendance and other school-related activities;
Herding (7.4 percent) domestic animals for grazing or bringing grass to
    tethered animals at home;
Leisure (7.0 percent) relaxing, playing and 'doing nothing' at home, or
    paying a visit to the local *denge* (beer house);
Housework (5.9 percent) including sweeping, fire-lighting, cleaning cooking
    utensils and washing clothes;
Collecting firewood (5.0 percent), which does not include the purchasing
    of paraffin and charcoal;

---

[1]The analysis is based upon careful observation of household members' activities and discussions with numerous individuals over an extended period. More specifically, the distribution of labour within households was obtained by having a (literate) member of each household carefully record on a daily basis the division of activities among household members. While not all households records covered the same length of time, comparability was not affected since I was primarily interested in percentage distributions by age, sex and parent/child relationships.

One problem that could not be totally resolved, however, was that of the comparability of activities in terms of time and effort. It is obvious, for instance, that fetching water would take less time than cultivating, or, for that matter, spending a day in school. Likewise, the amount of labour or skill involved in the different tasks could not be quantified. To overcome this problem, activities have been categorized under two umbrella-like categories. Hence an activity could be either predominantly productive in an accumulative or consumptive manner, or non-productive altogether. And within these two major categories, activities are listed under five themes which facilitate easy comparability. This comparability is further enhanced by my personal familiarity with the general way of life under investigation, and by constant checks on the accuracy of the records.

Visits and journeys (4.5 percent) involve being away from home for more
than one day on visits. Those away from home on account of being
employed elsewhere are not included here;

Cash labour (4.4 percent) includes the deployment of labour in any activity
whose immediate return is in cash form. The labour might be hired or
self-employed;

Milking (2.8 percent);

Errands (2.8 percent) including shopping and going to market;

Social duties (2.5 percent) including attending secular and religious
meetings, and formal and informal ceremonies;

Others (1.8 percent);

Illness (1.7 percent);

Child-minding (1.3 percent).

A household uses its labour for activities which are either predominantly
productive in an accumulative/consumptive manner or for activities which are
non-productive altogether. I have isolated five themes within this kind of
labour-utilization framework.

Essentially Accumulative Tasks (AT): A household engages its labour on these
activities primarily for the immediate procurement of its food and other
basic and pressing needs. It is under this category that a household is
expected to produce more than its own domestic requirements, to enable it to
participate in a wider economy. The following tasks fall into this
category: *shamba* work, herding, milking, cash labour and child-minding.
This last task is included because its major contributory function is in
releasing labour for productive work.

Essentially Consumption Tasks (CT): Under this category come the activities
which in one way or another have something to do with immediate consumption.
Such tasks include cooking, water-fetching, firewood-collecting, housework
and errands.

Essentially Socio-economic Investment Tasks (SIT): Social duties, visits and
journeys, school and any other activities which a household undertakes as an
investment for the future, all fall into this category. The education of a
household's children is naturally an important and concrete investment,
while the social links created through the undertaking of social duties,
visits and journeys, can prove useful in times of need.

Underutilized-labour Activities (ULA): Leisure and related activities are
found in this category. Much of the leisure is in fact forced upon the
respondents. For example, school-age children who cannot go to school
because of lack of money for school fees are usually found at home 'doing
nothing'. Theirs is forced 'leisure'. The same could be said of the rural
unemployed and underemployed.

Labour Wastage Activities (LWA): Illness is the main cause of labour wastage
in a household. Other causes are bereavement, laziness, etc.

There are three main variables which determine the division of labour within
a household, and these are sex, age and parent/child relationships. In
addition, cutting across these three variables there exist two collateral
ones, namely the household's hierarchical structure and the socio-economic
rank cum status of the task to be done within the household's total environment. There is in most cases a hierarchical element at work either at the
inter-strata or intra-strata levels in many given situations. The interplay
of the hierarchical element with the rank cum status of the task to be done

eventually determines the household's source of labour and the allocation of the various tasks and activities.

A study of the division of labour involves more than just the tabulation of the different tasks in male female or parent child, or whatever paradigms. It also entails the classification of tasks under the productive/non-productive dichotomy, listing them under their thematic categories and then superimposing these on the paradigms of the division of labour. It is a multifaceted approach whose basis is the three variables inherent in a household unit but always in a state of flux with the other two collateral ones. With this in mind, I attempt to illustrate how the mechanism of the division of labour operates at the household level. To do this, I show the first five activities in order of frequency, taking sex and parent/child relationships as the determining variables (Chart 8.1).[2]

Chart 8.1. Division of Labour by Parent/Child Relationship

	Tasks in order of frequency		Initials*	
	Parents	Children	Parents	Children
1.	Cooking	Cooking	CT	CT
2.	*Shamba* work	School	AT	SIT
3.	Cash labour	Water-fetching	AT	CT
4.	Leisure	Herding	ULA	AT
5.	Milking	Leisure	AT	ULA

*Key to relevant initials.

AT essentially accumulative tasks,
CT essentially consumption tasks,
SIT essentially socio-economic investment activities,
ULA underutilized labour activities,
LWA labour-wastage activities.

Out of the sample's total labour spent on carrying out the sixteen household activities, parents' and children's contributions formed 37 and 63 percent respectively. The children's contribution, which is almost double the parental one, is partly due to the fact that children outnumber their parents by 2:1. What the chart highlights is that parental labour is employed in tasks which are more accumulatively productive than child's labour and where parents contribute three times as much to these activities. Hence the parent's role as chief breadwinner seems at first sight to be vindicated. Chart 8.2 shows that the breadwinning role is mostly performed by male parents rather than female ones, with the latter engaged more in 'indoor' tasks than the former.

---

[2]Age has not been taken as an isolated variable for the purpose of these paradigms. The raw data was not collected on age basis. Nevertheless, the influence of age is reflected in the parent/child relationship and household hierarchical structure.

Chart 8.2.   Division of Labour of Parent Population by Sex

Tasks in order of frequency		Initials	
Male	Female	Male	Female
1. Cash labour	Cooking	AT	CT
2. *Shamba* work	*Shamba* work	AT	AT
3. Milking	Housework	AT	CT
4. Leisure	Social duties	ULA	SIT
5. Visits/journeys	Leisure	SIT	ULA

Hence, where the division of labour by sex is concerned, the preponderance of males being engaged more in accumulative activities (and thus fulfilling their expected breadwinning role) than females is shown in Chart 8.3.

Chart 8.3.   Division of Labour by Sex

Tasks in order of frequency		Initials	
Male	Female	Male	Female
1. School	Cooking	SIT	CT
2. Herding	Water-fetching	AT	CT
3. *Shamba* work	*Shamba* work	AT	AT
4. Cash labour	Housework	AT	CT
5. Leisure	School	ULA	SIT

Furthermore, the theme of parents being the breadwinners is maintained when it comes to the division of labour within the entire male population. Among the males, it is the father rather than the son who is engaged in the traditionally regarded breadwinning tasks. But the son's apprenticeship should not be overlooked (see Chart 8.4).

Chart 8.4.   Division of Labour of Male Population by Father/Son Relationship

Tasks in order of frequency		Initials	
Fathers	Sons	Fathers	Sons
1. Cash labour	School	AT	SIT
2. *Shamba* work	Herding	AT	AT
3. Milking	Water-fetching	AT	CT
4. Leisure	Leisure	ULA	ULA
5. Visits/journeys	Cooking	SIT	CT

However, one should not be led to conclude that men in general, and male
parents in particular, necessarily contribute more materially to the household's upkeep than females (see Chart 8.5).

Chart 8.5. Division of Labour of Female Population by
            Mother/Daughter Relationship

Tasks in order of frequency		Initials	
Mothers	Daughters	Mothers	Daughters
1. Cooking	Cooking	CT	CT
2. *Shamba* work	Water-fetching	AT	CT
3. Housework	School	CT	SIT
4. Social duties	Housework	SIT	CT
5. Leisure	*Shamba* work	ULA	AT

Indeed, these charts show that females – both mothers and daughters – are
constantly engaged in one activity or another with little rest in between
(they score two against the males' five leisure activities). The well-known
statement that in general women work more than men appears to be valid and,
according to Chart 8.5, for daughters more so than mothers.

These charts also indicate the importance of child labour and the supportive
and crucial role it plays within the household economy. Division of labour
within the child population stands out clearly when looked at from the sex
variable. It is the different levels of frequencies of the dominant themes
which bare the influence of sex in the division of labour process.

There is a tendency to regard the pursuit of investment and accumulative
activities in the form of schooling and herding as a main priority for male
children, as compared to consumption activities pursued by female children
(see Chart 8.6). This is worthy of note, especially since out of the
sample's school-age population of 65, there are 28 boys and 37 girls. In
theory girls should follow boys in placing schooling at the top of their
list. In practice only for boys is schooling the top priority which
manifests the latent importance parents attach to male children, and the
high status of men in Taita society in general.

Chart 8.6. Division of Labour of Child Population by Sex

Tasks in order of frequency		Initials	
Male	Female	Male	Female
1. School	Cooking	SIT	CT
2. Herding	Water-fetching	AT	CT
3. Water-fetching	School	CT	SIT
4. Leisure	Housework	ULA	CT
5. Cooking	*Shamba* work	CT	AT

In addition to the division of labour, there is also the distribution of
labour, which is mostly determined by the hierarchical social structure of a
household and the socio-economic rank cum status of the activity. The
percentage distribution of labour according to the five thematic activity
categories is as follows:

> 46 percent   CT (essentially consumption tasks),
> 27 percent   AT (essentially accumulative tasks),
> 18 percent   SIT (essentially socio-economic investment tasks),
> 7 percent   ULA (underutilizing labour activities),
> 2 percent   LWA (labour-wastage activities).

The influence of the hierarchical household social structure is borne out
when the percentages are allocated to the sex and parent/child variables of
division of labour (see Table 8.2).

Table 8.2. Distribution and Division of Labour According
to Sex and Parent/Child Relationship Within a
Household

Activities by initials	Male %	Female %	Parent %	Children %	Father %	Mother %	Father %	Son %	Mother %	Daughter %	Son %	Daughter %
CT	19	81	28	72	10	90	21	79	29	71	21	79
AT	53	47	56	44	51	49	56	44	58	42	54	46
SIT	46	54	25	75	41	59	22	78	27	73	48	52
ULA	47	53	39	61	48	52	41	59	38	62	46	54
LWA	16	84	81	19	11	89	53	47	86	14	40	60
Average	41	59	37	63	38	62	35	65	38	62	42	58

In the hierarchical social structure of the household, the socio-cultural
status of a woman is lower than that of a man; a mother's status is lower
than a father's; a son's lower than a father's; a daughter's lower than a
mother's; and a daughter's lower than a son's. By taking the three top
important groups of activities, namely consumption, accumulation and investment, either singly or by pairing them or by aggregating all three, one finds
that the person(s) whose status is lower than the rest contributes more to
the activities to be done, with the exception of the high status accumulation
tasks where parents and especially men contribute more. Where sons and
daughters are concerned when it comes to doing investment activities, this
generalization does not hold if the activities are considered singly;
nevertheless, it is operative in the other situations, namely pairing and
aggregating. Even within this exception, where sons contribute 48 percent
and daughters 52 percent, the difference in quality and quantity of labour
so contributed needs to be borne in mind. For the son's contribution is
more in the form of schooling and herding, while the daughter's contribution
is more in the form of social duties, visits and journeys.

It can be found that for the three most important activities, labour contributions are as follows:

Father	33.5 percent,
Mother	52.0 percent,
Son	54.0 percent,
Daughter	60.5 percent.

From the analysis of the ways in which a household utilizes its labour, two sets of trends are particularly noteworthy. Firstly, that in its distribution, household labour is spent more on consumption than production-orientated activities. Secondly, in the division of labour, males work less than females, sons work less than daughters, and fathers work less than mothers. Similarly, parents work less than children, fathers work less than sons and mothers work less than daughters.

Hence, where division of labour is concerned, it is good to be a male and best of all to be a husband and father. Conversely, it is bad to be a female and worst of all a daughter.[3]

Having examined the division of labour, its distribution and utilization at the household level, I now intend to analyse the same phenomenon at the inter-strata level. Inter-strata comparative analysis rests on a socio-economic base, with the added advantage that it offers the opportunity for each individual stratum to be treated as a case study.

Stratum One consists of thirty-six people, eight of whom are parents: four fathers and four mothers. Of the twenty-eight children, fourteen are sons, thirteen daughters and one is a granddaughter.

None of the parents have salaried employment, although three of the male parents have skills such as masonry and carpentry and in addition a little knowledge of reading and writing. There being little demand for their skills, they are in most cases hired to do various jobs such as portage, sand-scooping[4] or any kind of *kibarua* (casual job). One of the male parents is a *de jure* but not *de facto* head of his family, for he is permanently settled in the lowlands, ostensibly working as a herdsman. But the fact is that it is his awareness of his inability to fend for his household that has made him abrogate his *de facto* responsibility.

None of the women have salaried employment. They are engaged in producing food on their *shambas*.

Of the fourteen male children, three are casual labourers - one in Mombasa and two in Taita. Of the remaining eleven, seven are at school, two have dropped out because of lack of school fees, and three are still very young.

Of the female children, one is an adult and divorcee with a young daughter, five are in primary school, two are not going to school because of lack of school fees, and four are still very young.

---

[3] A comparative study of a Javanese village and a Nepalese village comes to a similar conclusion that girls overall contribute more to household work than boys (see Nag *et al.*, 1977).

[4] The finer silt in the river beds is scooped and used for making bricks.

Stratum Two has twenty-eight people, ten of whom are married adults. Of the remaining eighteen, five are male and thirteen are female children.

The adult population is made up of four fathers, four mothers, a married son and daughter-in-law. Two of the fathers have salaried employment, one in Taita on a poultry farm and the other as a cook in an institution in Nairobi. Of the remaining two fathers, one is a local lumberjack and carpenter by training, although his skills are not always in demand. The other is over 60 and has abandoned practising as a herbalist since his conversion to a Christian sect. His married son was recently made redundant; he has also been converted to his father's sect.

None of the women have salaried employment, but work on their *shambas*. Two of them - the cook's and lumberjack's wives - are involved in organizing other women for self-improvement activities such as raising funds for putting up good houses.

Of the five sons, two are in primary school, two are employed in Mombasa and one is unemployed. As for the girls, two have finished their primary education and are unmarried and unemployed, seven are still at school (three in secondary and four in primary), while the remaining four are below school-going age.

Stratum Three has the biggest population: forty-one people altogether. It has an adult population of thirteen people, six of whom are parents - two husbands, two wives and two widows. Of the remaining seven adults, there are three sons (one of whom is married), a daughter-in-law and two unmarried daughters.

Of the parent population, only one has salaried employment. This is the sub-chief of the area; he has no grown-up children. The rest are actively engaged in producing food from their *shambas*, and their income is supplemented by earnings from their employed children. One of the widows rents out houses and a sewing machine. She obtained the initial capital from an insurance company as reimbursement for the death of her husband, who was killed in a road accident. The other widow has two working sons, one (the married one) as a teacher (deputy headmaster) and one as a lorry driver. Her daughter-in-law was at the time of research in a teacher training college. The two unmarried daughters are both employed in Mombasa as housemaids, while their brother works on the *shamba* with their parents.

Of the child population, twelve are male and seventeen female. Of the male children, one is in nursery school, eight in primary school and two in secondary school. Only one male child is under school age. Of the female children, two are in nursery school, twelve in primary school, two are primary graduates and so far unmarried and unemployed; one is not old enough to go to school.

Stratum Four has the smallest population, with twenty-seven people. The adult population consists of one grandmother and eight parents - four husbands and four wives. These last eight are all employed in petty agro-business or in big commercial ventures. The husbands and wives have close working relationships and one of the wives manages a shop, jointly owned with her husband.

The 'dependent' child population is made up of nine male and nine female children. Of the male children, one is too young to go to school, two are in nursery, three are in primary and three are in secondary school. As for the girls, four are too young to go to school, one is in nursery, three are in primary and one in secondary school.

I have already indicated that 59 percent of the sample's labour supply is made up of females (see Table 8.2). Table 8.3 shows that the division of labour is not only determined by sex but also by the socio-economic stratum of the household.

Table 8.3.   Division of Labour by Sex and Strata

Strata	Percentages	
	Male	Female
One	34	66
Two	29	71
Three	34	66
Four*	52	48

*Ten percent of the labour in this stratum comes from hired labourers - 6 percent females and 4 percent males.

With the exception of Stratum Four, Table 8.3 shows that females work harder than men. As for Stratum Four, I try to show that it is not in every situation that females work less. One way of doing this is by giving the first five activities in order of frequency according to strata and sex (see Chart 8.7).

Chart 8.7.   Activities in Order of Frequency According to Stratum and Sex

Sex	Activities in order of frequency	Strata							
		One		Two		Three		Four	
M	1	Cash labour	AT	Milking	AT	Herding	AT	School	SIT
A	2	Shamba work	AT	Herding	AT	School	SIT	Shamba work	AT
L	3	Herding	AT	School	SIT	Water-fetching	CT	Cash labour	AT
E									
S	4	Social labour		Cooking	CT	Shamba work	AT	Leisure	ULA
	5	Leisure	ULA	Visits and journeys	SIT	Leisure	ULA	Errands	CT
F	1	Cooking	CT	Cooking	CT	Cooking	CT	School	SIT
E	2	Housework	CT	Water-fetching	CT	School	SIT	Cooking	CT
M									
A	3	Shamba work	AT	Shamba work	AT	Water-fetching	CT	Firewood	CT
L	4	Visits and journeys	SIT	Visits and journeys	SIT	Shamba work	AT	Shamba work	AT
E									
S	5	Leisure	ULA	Housework	CT	Housework	CT	Water-fetching	CT

The diversity of division of labour based on sex becomes vivid when looked at from inter- and intra-strata levels; no two strata or sexes place activities in identical order of frequency. It should, of course, be borne in mind that both the parent/child ratio and the sex ratio are unequal within any one stratum, and furthermore the degree of 'unequalness' varies from stratum to stratum. That the strata apparently perform similar activities does not minimize the socio-economic differentiation existing among them. This underlying source of differentiation is manifested in the way each stratum places the activities in a different order of frequency, and in so doing gives an indication of priority within the notion of frequency. For example, in Chart 8.7 school does not feature at all in Stratum One, while in Stratum Two it is in third place for males, in Stratum Three it is in second place for both sexes and in Stratum Four it is the top activity for both sexes. The socio-economic differentiation is more accentuated when the four strata are collapsed into two - poor and rich - and then listing and comparing their five top activities (Chart 8.8).

Chart 8.8.   First Five Activities of the Four Strata

Activities in order of frequency	Strata							
	One		Two		Three		Four	
1	Cooking	CT	Cooking	CT	Cooking	CT	School	SIT
2	Cash labour	AT	Water-fetching	CT	Herding	AT	*Shamba* work	AT
3	*Shamba* work	CT	*Shamba* work	AT	Water-fetching	CT	Cash labour	AT
4	Housework	CT	Visits and journeys	SIT	School	SIT	Water-fetching	CT
5	Visits and journeys	SIT	Milking	AT	*Shamba* work	AT	Leisure	ULA

Chart 8.9 shows that the poor concentrate their labour on production-consumption activities, while the rich place more emphasis on production-accumulative activities. Although both the poor and rich are engaged in socio-economic investment activities, the poor seem to participate more in the social aspects of this category (here represented in the form of visits and journeys) than the rich, who seem to stress the economic component (here represented in the form of sending their children to school).

Chart 8.9.   First Five Activities of the Rich and Poor

	Poor strata	Symbols	Rich strata	Symbols
1.	Cooking	CT	School	SIT
2.	*Shamba* work	AT	Cooking	CT
3.	Water-fetching	CT	Water-fetching	CT
4.	Visits/journeys	SIT	*Shamba* work	AT
5.	Housework	CT	Herding	AT

Chart 8.8 indicates that the activities done by Stratum Four come close to an ideal situation of the way a household can utilize its labour in its efforts towards economic development. The activities and their order of frequency tell a story in which investment (and here it is investment in education) goes hand in hand with surplus generating activities on the *shamba* and from other sources. It is only subsequently that consumption and leisure activities are pursued.

The poor strata waste more labour than the rich. The main cause of labour wastage among the household members of the sample is ill health. There might be a temptation to see a causal relationship between the socio-economic conditions of the sample and the general state of health of its members. While ill-health does contribute to labour wastage, there exists another subtle contributory factor: household disciplinary management.

With children being a major source of labour, the harnessing of this source depends on how the household is managed. A household which finds itself short of labour, whether it be through disciplinary mismanagement, ill-health or schooling, might cover the deficit by hiring labour. But I have already shown that it is only Stratum Four which is in a position to hire labour (either on a casual or permanent basis) and even so, hired labour provides only 10 percent of the stratum's total labour force (see Table 8.3 above).

The disciplining of children largely depends on the socio-economic conditions prevailing in a household. It is very difficult for parents to obtain co-operation from their growing children if they cannot feed and clothe them adequately or pay for their school fees. Harsh circumstances force children to learn how to fend for themselves and even become the household's bread-winners at an early age (see Chart 8.10). As a result, parents become reluctant to impose discipline in the short run because doing so would mean trying to turn a self-reliant child who is not costing much into a dependent child who they are unable to support anyway. However, in the long run, this means that children from poorer families tend not to be in a position to contribute substantially to the general upkeep of the household, in contrast to children from richer families where schooling is a top priority.

With this argument in mind, I now turn to an examination of how children in the different strata contribute their labour.

Children's Contribution to the Household's Upkeep

Children[5] supply 63 percent of the sample's total labour spent on the different activities. But not all strata enjoy such a high labour contribution from their children.

Looking at Table 8.4, one is struck by the low labour contribution of the children in Stratum One. The age variable could offer an explanation. Table 8.5 shows the average ages of the household heads of each stratum and of the children in each stratum. The average age of the former seems to correspond with that of the latter within the same stratum. For example, Stratum Two is the 'oldest' and has the 'oldest' children; it is followed by Stratum Three, with Stratum One and Four being the 'youngest', but with One

---

[5]Children here include the adult sons, unmarried daughters and daughters-in-law of the household head, since they are in a single household.

having 'younger' children than Four. The average age difference between
children in One and Four is just 2 years. However, Table 8.4 shows a big
difference in labour contributed by the two groups of children to their
respective strata. There is also a 2-year difference between the children
in Strata Two and Three, but it is worth noting that the 'younger' children
in Three contribute 17 percent more labour than their 'older' counterparts
in Two. Finally, it is worth noting that the average age of children in
Strata One and Two combined (the poor strata) and Strata Three and Four
combined (the rich strata) is the same - 11 years. And yet, as Table 8.4
shows, children from the rich strata contribute as much as 28 percent more
labour to their households than their counterparts in the poor strata.
This difference in labour contribution cannot be attributed to the numerical
advantage of the rich strata alone, since this is only 4 percent (there are
fifty-two and forty-eight children in the rich and poor strata respectively).
While numeracy has a contributory effect, it cannot be regarded as a
deciding factor. The same applies where the age variable is concerned.[6]

Table 8.4.   Contribution of Labour by Children to their
             Respective Strata

Strata	One	Two	Three	Four
Percentage of labour supplied by children	18%	62%	79%	62%
Number of children	28	20	34	18
Number of children as percentage of stratum's total population	75%	72%	83%	66%

Table 8.5.   Average Ages of Household Heads and of
             Children by Stratum

Strata	Average age of household heads	Average age of children
One	36	8
Two	44	14
Three	40	12
Four	36	10

[6] I am not refuting the thesis propounded by Chayanov that the age of a family
determines its population size and therefore its source of labour and
development potential in peasant economies. What I am stressing is the
mechanism by which a household harnesses the labour force at its disposal;
and my argument is that, with all other things being equal, this mechanism
is intertwined with a household's socio-economic level. For Chayanov's
thesis, see Shanin, 1971: 150-159.

Instead, from my own in-depth knowledge of the families concerned, I would argue that the labour contributed by children is heavily dictated by the household disciplinary management factor, which in turn depends largely on the socio-economic level of the household.

It now remains to examine the type of activities done by children (Chart 8.10).

Chart 8.10.   First Five Activities done by Children
              of Different Strata

Activities in order of frequency	Strata							
	One		Two		Three		Four	
1	Cash labour	AT	Cooking	CT	Cooking	CT	School	SIT
2	Herding	AT	Water-fetching	CT	Water-fetching	CT	Water-fetching	CT
3	Water-fetching	CT	*Shamba* work	AT	Herding	AT	Leisure	ULA
4	School	SIT	Visits and journeys	SIT	School	SIT	Firewood	CT
5	*Shamba* work	AT	School	SIT	Housework	CT	Cooking	CT

Children in Stratum One seem to be engaged more in breadwinning activities than children in the other strata. This is in general true of the children in the poor strata compared to those in the rich strata. It is also interesting to note that children in Stratum One are engaged in cash labour (indeed, they rank it first), while it does not feature at all in the activities done by children in the other strata. The type of work done by children under cash labour is casual labouring. This further substantiates what I have already said about how children from poor households learn to fend for themselves and even become the household's breadwinners at an early age.

On the other hand, there are more opportunities open to children from the rich strata than to those in the poor strata. In this connection, it is interesting to note the frequency order schooling is given by each stratum. It is placed fourth by Stratum One, fifth by Stratum Two, fourth by Stratum Three and first by Stratum Four. The relative advantage children from the rich strata have over those from the poor strata stands out more clearly when the sex variable is introduced (see Chart 8.11).

Division of labour based on prescribed sex roles seems to be confirmed by the choices of activities for the children. For example, boys do the herding while girls do the cooking. In general, boys do more of the outdoor activities while girls do more of the indoor ones. Such specialization based on sex is more pronounced in the first three strata. In Stratum Four activities seem to have been 'de-gendered', or are in the process of being so, thus putting male and female children from this stratum on an equal footing. Hence the symbiotic relationship existing between males and females in the form of division of labour is becoming more utilitarian in the richest stratum, but remaining culture-bound in the relatively poorer strata. This is especially true where school is concerned.

Chart 8.11. Activities done by Children, by Strata and Sex

Sex	Activities in order of frequency	Strata							
		One		Two		Three		Four	
M	1	Cash labour	AT	School	SIT	Herding	AT	School	SIT
A	2	Herding	AT	Herding	AT	School	SIT	Errands	CT
L	3	School	SIT	Cooking	CT	Water-fetching	CT	Water-fetching	CT
E									
S	4	Illness	LAT	Visits and journeys	SIT	Leisure	ULA	Leisure	ULA
	5	Water-fetching	CT	Water-fetching	CT	Cooking	CT	Cooking	CT
F	1	Water-fetching	CT	Cooking	CT	Cooking	CT	School	SIT
E									
M	2	School	SIT	Water-fetching	CT	Water-fetching	CT	Firewood	CT
A	3	Shamba work	AT	Shamba work	AT	School	SIT	Water-fetching	CT
L									
E	4	Leisure	ULA	Visits and journeys	SIT	Housework	CT	Leisure	ULA
S	5	Cooking	CT	Housework	CT	Shamba work	AT	Cooking	CT

The place of *shamba* work highlights differentiation based on the socio-economic variable at inter-strata level, and the interaction of this variable with the sex roles. That the fulcrum of the household economy lies in this activity is confirmed by the way all the strata locate it high on their frequency order (taking the whole sample, adults and children, into consideration). Usually, it comes immediately after consumption and investment activities, which need to be done regularly and frequently. They are also, in most cases, activities done by children whose population is larger than the parents'. This notwithstanding, the location of *shamba* work in third place on the frequency list emphasizes the significant role it plays in the household economy. Of the total labour the sample used on accumulative activities, 40 percent is allocated to *shamba* work and each stratum, in ascending order, ranks it third, third, fifth and second respectively.

Shamba work features among the top five activities done by children from the poor strata but not among those done by children from the rich strata. In Stratum One, female children rank it third and male children seventh (see Appendix IV). In Stratum Two it is ranked third and eighth by female and male children respectively. In Stratum Three it is ranked fifth and sixth by females and males respectively. This indicates that socialization towards male and female roles is well established at an early stage.[7] As for Stratum Four, the contribution to *shamba* work is not very significant and is included under the 'Others' category of activities. This further illustrates how children from the rich strata work less on such activities in the short run.

---

[7]As a matter of comparison, starting from Stratum One, male parents rank *shamba* work 2nd, 7th, 1st and 2nd, respectively; and female parents rank it 3rd, 4th, 1st and 2nd, respectively.

Taking population as a labour resource, I have attempted in this chapter to illuminate the following points.

Firstly, the inevitable dependence of the household on labour from children and the consequent interdependence between parents and children. Secondly, the distribution of household labour is firstly determined by culturally rooted sex-specific tasks as well as by the household's self-disciplinary managerial capability, which sets the activities to be done in priority order and enforces the mechanism of the division of labour. Finally, the options open to a household in the way it exploits its labour largely depend on the household's socio-economic status.

The next chapter attempts to show whether the utilization of this labour on the household *shamba* does in fact provide the basic necessity - a sufficient food supply for the household.

CHAPTER 9

Food Production, Consumption and Cash Expenditure

This chapter examines one primary question: do the households produce enough food to meet their own internal consumption needs? The failure or success of land reform should be judged only according to whether or not the peasants have enough to eat the whole year round. In attempting to answer this question I use the data from my sixteen sample households.[1]

---

[1]Each of the sample households was asked to fill in a form entitled *Food Consumption and Expenses per Household*. Horizontally it was divided into four sections:

Section A: Chakula, which concerns itself with *chakula*, which literally translates as 'food', but is in actual fact used to refer to the basic food, which in Taita is usually *ugali*, made from maize-meal. There are five kinds of basic foods listed under this section and an extra column for 'others'.

Section B: Mboga, which relates to *mboga* - i.e. 'relish' - which is the complementary dish to *chakula*. Nine varieties are listed with an extra column for 'others'. For the Taita meal only becomes complete when there is *chakula* and *mboga*.

Section C: Source of foodstuffs required the household to state the source of the foodstuffs which make up *chakula* and *mboga*. The main sources are the *shamba*, shop and market. If the food comes from the *shamba*, I refer to it as home produced; and whenever cash is involved in getting the food - usually from the shop or market - it is categorized as purchased. The money spent on purchased food was also recorded.

Section D: Number of people sharing a meal, where the household was required to record the number of people who sat down to eat each meal. Here I initially met resistance from the respondents because, according to Kitaita custom, counting people before or after a meal is a sign of bad manners and outright meanness especially so if there is a visitor. Whenever a visitor was present, counting was done discreetly. But eventually this practice was abandoned by households, who explained their strange behaviour by quoting me as the main source of it. This was easily understood because I was known as "that man who goes round asking funny questions".

[*Footnote continued opposite*]

Of the home-produced *chakula*, 58 percent is produced and consumed by the rich strata; the poor strata produce and consume the remaining 42 percent with the poorest stratum producing and consuming the least. Conversely, of the purchased *chakula*, 62 percent of it is purchased by the poor strata, with the poorest stratum buying the most; the rich strata buy the remaining 38 percent, the richest stratum buying the least (see Table 9.1).

Evening meals comprised 52 percent (493) of the total 948 meals taken. Home-produced *chakula* comprised 63 percent of the total *chakula* taken, while the remaining 37 percent was purchased (see Table 9.2).

Vertically the form is divided into days, with each day being subdivided to account for the two main meals of the day - the midday meal and the evening meal. Another form for breakfast was also circulated, but these data are not included here.

A separate form titled *Daily Household Expenditure* was used to record the daily purchase made by the household, apart from basic foods. The participants were required to write down the amount of money they spent against the items purchased. Thus the total daily household expenditure is computed from the money spent on *chakula* and *mboga* plus the separate daily expenditure form.

Household members were asked to fill in the form themselves, and it did not take long for those who could read and write to learn how to complete it daily.

The data gathering covered a 4-month period, although none of the households were involved for the whole period. This meant the problems of boredom and resultant slackness among the participants in recording this information were avoided. The distribution of the forms to the households was staggered in such a way as to create a wider socio-economic catchment area within such a duration.

Food consumption habits at the beginning and end of the month tend to differ from those in the middle of the month. They also differed according to the agricultural cycle, the various geographical zones and according to whether a household is relatively rich or poor. The staggering was therefore designed so that at any one time, households representing all four strata were actively involved in the data gathering.

For the purpose of analysis, the data thus gathered for the entire 4-month period has been condensed and standardized to cover a period of a 30 days month. Thus, assuming that each household has two main meals a day, the potential total for the whole month would be sixty meals per household, or 960 for the whole sample.

When a meal has been eaten by fewer people than the constant population of the household, I have called it a 'meal-absence' phenomenon. And when a household shared its meal with more people than its own members, I have termed this a 'meal-presence' phenomenon (see p.106).

Consumption Pattern

The sample's consumption of meals during the period of analysis totalled 948, which is twelve meals short of the potential 960. Of the meals taken, 48 percent (455) were midday meals. Of these midday meals, 74 percent of the *chakula* supplies came from the *shamba* (i.e. they were home-produced), while the rest (26 percent) came from the shop or market (i.e. they were purchased). The next question is, how are these *chakula* supplies distributed among the four strata?

Table 9.1.　Midday Meal *Chakula* Sources by Stratum
　　　　　　(in percentages)

Strata	Percentage of sample	*Chakula* sources			
		Home-produced		Purchased	
One	28	16	}42	39	}62
Two	21	26		23	
Three	31	30	}58	25	}38
Four	20	28		13	
Total	100.0	100.0		100.0	

Table 9.2.　Evening Meal *Chakula* Sources by Stratum
　　　　　　(in percentages)

Strata	Percentage of sample	*Chakula* sources			
		Home-produced		Purchased	
One	28	21	}45	35	}60
Two	21	24		25	
Three	31	27	}55	26	}40
Four	20	28		14	
Total	100.0	100.0		100.0	

The rich strata produce and consume 55 percent of the home-produced *chakula* and the poor strata 45 percent with the poorest producing and consuming the least.　Of the purchased *chakula*, 60 percent is bought by the poor strata, with the poorest buying the most.　The rich strata buy the remaining 40 percent, with the richest stratum buying the least.

For the whole sample, home-produced *chakula* comprised 68 percent and purchased *chakula* 32 percent of the total *chakula* supplies consumed.　The rich strata's share of the home-produced *chakula* makes up 39 percent, compared with the poor strata's 29 percent and the rich strata's share of purchased *chakula* makes up 13 percent while the poor strata's share is 19 percent.　Hence households in the rich strata produce most of their *chakula* supplies and buy little, while households in the poor strata produce less of their *chakula* supplies and therefore have to buy most of it.　Here, it might be remembered from the previous chapter that households in the poor strata have smaller average holdings than households in the rich strata.

However, the above generalizations concern *chakula* only.　The situation is quite the reverse when it comes to the supplies for the complementary dish *mboga*, which together with *chakula* make up a full meal.

Households in the rich strata consumed less home-produced *mboga* than their counterparts in the poor strata. This is not because of the rich households' inability to grow their own supplies, but rather because of their ability to buy better quality *mboga* relative to other households. In general, meat *mboga* carries a higher status than any *mboga* produced on the *shamba*.

However, this observation needs to be qualified, since home-produced *mboga* has two functions, subsistence and cash. Subsistence *mboga* has two components: the foraging and gathering of weed-like plants known as *munyunya* and various kinds of *munavu*, which grow wild locally; secondly, the cultivation of certain crops primarily for domestic consumption (although the produce might be sold for cash in times of dire need or because there is a surplus). These *mboga* crops are in most cases pulses such as *maharagwe* (red kidney beans) and *pojo* (mung beans). The cash function of home-produced *mboga* entails the cultivation of market-garden type vegetables primarily for the market (although the household might use some for its own *mboga*). The main vegetables grown for cash are cabbages, *sukumawiki* (leafy cabbage), lettuce, spinach, carrots and tomatoes.

One way in which land individualization has transformed the peasant way of life and economy is manifested by the penetration of the cash economy into the foraging and gathering of *munyunya* and *munavu*. Prior to the land reform, such weeds grew wild, and could be collected free by anyone who needed them for *mboga*, even if they were growing in someone else's *shamba*. While this type of *mboga* still grows wild on people's *shamba's*, private land ownership has ended the old communal arrangement of gathering it freely. The new practice is to gather and harvest this wild-growing *mboga* from one's own *shamba* and then sell it at the local market to those who are unable to afford the more expensive types of *mboga*, such as beef, mutton, goat meat, vegetables and pulses. Thus the obliteration of the foraging and gathering section within the subsistence component of the home-produced *mboga* calls for rapid adaptation on the part of the poor peasantry.

To reiterate, a meal is complete only when there are both *chakula* and *mboga*, usually each being prepared as a separate dish. For example, *chakula* might be maize-meal or rice and this might be eaten with *munavu*, beans or beef as *mboga*. On other occasions, however, maize and beans are cooked together into a mash called *kimanga*. Whatever the method of preparation, the texture, taste and nutritional value of the meal depends on the ingredients used. As I have already shown, the procurement of these foodstuffs depends on the household's socio-economic status, and *mboga* consumption easily mirrors this differentiation.

It comes as no surprise therefore to find that the low status, poorer-quality *shamba*-produced *mboga* is consumed more by the poorer households. The ratio of consumption of *shamba*-produced *mboga* by the poor strata and the rich strata is 5:3.

The *mboga* role of pulses, especially *maharagwe*, is diffuse from approximately June to November because June to August is the harvest period and, depending on the size of the yield, many a household's supply is already depleted or becoming so towards the end of the year. Another reason for this diffuseness is that immediately after the harvest, pulses provide the basis for many kinds of *kimanga* dishes. But towards the end of September, the *mboga* role of these pulses becomes more consistent because of scarcity. The peasants now tend to economize by cooking the beans as a separate dish rather than as a richer *kimanga* dish. It is at this time that a household's consumption of pulses, in particular *maharagwe*, is determined in most cases by the amount of cash it has at its disposal. Thus invariably, households in the poor strata find themselves having *maharagwe* less frequently and resorting more and more to *munyunya* and *munavu* for their *mboga*.

The socio-economic differentiation is even more vivid when it comes to the consumption of purchased *mboga*. For example, the ratio of beef consumption by households in the poor strata and those in the rich strata is 5:12. In fact the poor peasant might eat meat as little as once a week or even once a month.

Having looked at the distribution of *chakula* and *mboga* supplies, I now intend to show further how the consumption pattern emerging out of this reality mirrors the socio-economic differentiation taking place at the grassroots level.

For this analysis, the economic function of a household as a consumption as well as a production unit is taken as given. A household is a production unit if it embodies one or a combination of the following sources of labour supply: parent or parents, employed sons or daughters, unemployed sons or daughters (since they work on the *shamba*) and lastly hired labour.

A consumption unit might include some or all the features found in a production unit. Usually there are more consumers than producers. As one saying puts it, "there is one cultivator but many eaters". In the case of a household member working in an urban area or elsewhere away from home, he or she is regarded as a member of the production unit but not of the consumption unit. His or her monthly visits home are regarded as enlarging the core consumption unit, while his/her absence stabilizes it.

The absence from a meal by a member of the consumption core ('meal-absence') may be explained by going without food, especially at lunch time; for instance, school children from the poorer households miss meals frequently at midday; similarly visits to neighbours or relatives, or a job which absents a member from the midday meal, or an extended business visit may also account for absences. Finally, of course, there is the possibility of going without food because it is not available.

Table 9.3 shows the distribution of the meal-absence phenomenon at inter-strata level (where the total meal-absenting done is 100 percent).

Table 9.3. Meal-absence by Stratum (in percentages)

Strata	Percentage of sample	Midday meal	Evening meal
One	28	53	29
Two	21	31	43
Three	31	6	8
Four	20	10	20
Total	100	100	100

The introduction of the socio-economic variables brings out the following points. Firstly, the poor strata are more often absent from meals than the rich strata. Secondly, whatever the meal, there is more meal-absence among the poor strata than the rich strata. For example, for the midday meal, meal absence is 84 percent for the poor strata and only 16 percent for the rich strata, while for the evening meal it is 72 percent and 28 percent for the poor and rich strata respectively. Thirdly, among the poor strata there is more meal-absence at the midday meal than at the evening meal. Lastly, among the rich strata, there is more meal-absence at the evening meal (28 percent) than at the midday meal (16 percent). Meal-absence among the rich strata is in most cases due to jobs and extended business visits undertaken by household members.

While the meal-absence phenomenon leads to the contraction of the household's core consumption unit, meal-presence, on the other hand, leads to either its stabilization or enlargement. This depends on whether those sharing the meal are core members, when the core consumption unit is thus stabilized, or non-core members and visitors, when the consumption unit is enlarged. The core's stabilization can only be achieved if the core members are not absent and non-core members and visitors are not present at meals. In reality it is almost impossible to have the core consumption unit stabilized. Its enlargement can be caused by the periodic homecoming of productive helpers (non-core members); meal-sharing with parents and relatives who are not household members; meal sharing with visitors or meal sharing with employees, especially casual labourers.

The following points can be deduced from Table 9.4: Of the total meal-presence phenomenon, over three-quarters takes place in the rich strata. Meal-presence among the rich strata is in most cases due to meal-sharing with visitors and employees, the latter being the case especially where Stratum Four is concerned. Irrespective of the meal, most of the meal-presence occurs in the rich strata. At the midday meal it is 98 percent for the rich strata and 2 percent for the poor strata, while at the evening meal it is 56 percent and 44 percent respectively. The rich strata have more extra mouths to feed at the midday meal than at the evening meal. This confirms the already mentioned observation that most meal-absence occurs among the poor strata, and that it occurs more at midday than in the evening. A manifestation of this pattern is the 42 percent rise in the meal-presence among the poor strata at the evening meal and the 42 percent decrease on the rich strata's side.

Table 9.4. Meal Presence by Stratum (in percentages)

Strata	Percentage of sample	Midday meal	Evening meal
One	28	*	31
Two	21	2	13
Three	31	7	4
Four	20	91	52
Total	100	100	100

*This means that no non-core members are present.

The 42 percent rise in the meal-presence occurring in the poor strata at the evening meal and the phenomenal increase of 31 percent in the poorest, Stratum One, is usually due to the homecoming of non-core members and meal-sharing with relatives. But this increase also portends the emergence of a one-meal day among the households in the poor strata.

This meal-absence/presence framework of food consumption indicates a pattern of horizontal and vertical relationships. At the horizontal level, consumers move to households which are situated within the socio-economic stratum to which they belong. With most of the movement within the meal-absence/presence phenomenon being done by members of the poor strata, their horizontal movement succeeds in reinforcing their mutual dependency relationships - or what can be aptly regarded as the poor sharing poverty among themselves.

At the vertical level, consumers are engaged in trans-strata movement, and since this movement is from the poor to the rich strata it inevitably leads to a patron-client relationship (although the ideology of kinship and tribalism may be used to camouflage it). The manifestation of this is in the relatively large out-flow from the poor strata in the meal-absence phenomenon and the corresponding in-flow into the rich strata in the meal-presence phenomenon. Indeed, despite the relative decrease in the in-flow of consumers at the evening meal, overall the rich strata, especially Stratum Four, seem to cater for a fairly constant number of extra consumers at both meals. Those sharing the meals might be friends, relatives, visitors and employees, but whatever the relationship it succeeds in generating a patron-client pattern which is exemplified by the constant meal-presence in-flow into the rich strata.

Cash Expenditure

Within the survey period, the sample's total cash expenditure was 9970.85 Kenya shillings (which is equivalent to Stg. £712.20).[2] The money was spent on the following items. Education (school fees and other contributions) accounted for 31 percent of the entire expenditure; 'luxuries' (cigarettes, alcohol, soft drinks, cosmetics and miscellanies such as clothes and condiments) for 26 percent; 'necessities' (tea,[3] sugar, toiletries, cooking-fat, paraffin and salt) amounted to 25 percent; and food (*chakula* and *mboga* ingredients) made up the remainder of the total expenditure.

How much importance people attach to the education of their children is shown by the fact that almost one-third of the total cash expenditure goes towards education.[4] But not every household spends proportionately the same on it (see Table 9.5).

_____

[2]At the time of writing, the exchange rate for £1 sterling is K 14 shillings.

[3]While coffee is grown as a cash crop, tea is the popular drink and has to be bought from shops.

[4]In fact, it has become a national craze. Since independence (1963) the Government has been allocating an increasing proportion of its expenditure to education; and if this trend were to continue at the same rate, by 1980, 80 percent of the annual budget would be spent on education alone (1974/78 Plan: 407). While the Government is now cutting down on its expenditure, it is doubtful if households will follow suit. Indeed with job opportunities receding, the chase after academic qualifications becomes more urgent than ever.

Table 9.5. Expenditure on Education by Stratum

Strata	% of sample	No. of dependent children	No. of school-aged children	No. of actual attenders	Amount in K. shillings	% of money spent
One	28	24	17	12*	36.60	1
Two	21	13	9	9	541.80	18
Three	31	27	25	25	937.00	31
Four	20	18	13	13	1537.90	50
Total	100	82	64	59	3047.30	100

*The five non-attenders have dropped out because of lack of school fees.

The relative ability of the rich peasants to pay for the education of their children is shown by the fact that 81 percent of the total expenditure on this item comes from the rich strata. This confirms what has already been mentioned that school is a top activity for children from the rich strata. It is not lack of school-age children but lack of money which is the main reason for the poor strata's dismal expenditure on education - especially the poorest.

The classical consumption pattern of the rich indulging in luxuries seems to hold good also for the sample Taita households (see Table 9.6).

Table 9.6. Household Expenditure on Luxuries by Stratum

Strata	Percentage of sample	Amount in K. shillings	Percentage
One	28	114.60	5
Two	21	677.70	26
Three	31	862.95	33
Four	20	924.80	36
Total	100	2580.05	100

The exceptional expenditure on necessities by the poor strata (see Table 9.7) is a deficit expenditure, this being most true where Stratum One is concerned. There is, however, little chance that the deficit will ever be cleared by the poor. One explanation of this is that in such a 'face to face' society, money-lending carries less of its economistic rationale. It operates within a web of kinship ties and obligations and also patron-client relationships, and creditors regard their debtors more in social than in economic terms.

Table 9.7.   Household Expenditure on Necessities by Stratum

Strata	Percentage of sample	Amount in K. shillings	Percentage
One	28	929.50	37
Two	21	427.60	17
Three	31	589.40	23
Four	20	581.25	23
Total	100	2527.75	100

That the poor strata appear to spend most of their cash income on basic needs is further shown by their 61 percent share of the sample's food purchases (see Table 9.8). During this period of data-gathering (April/May - August) *shamba*-produced food supplies in the poor households were either depleted or near to depletion, while households in the rich strata were still relying on their own supplies. This is evidenced by the fact that almost two-thirds of total expenditure on food was incurred by the poor strata. And again, much of this expenditure was deficit.

Table 9.8.   Household Food Purchases by Stratum

Strata	Percentage of sample	Amount in K. shillings	Percentage
One	28	645.05	36
Two	21	453.25	25
Three	31	348.80	19
Four	20	368.65	20
Total	100	1815.75	100

On the other hand, the rich households' self-sufficiency in food production is illustrated by their proportionately smaller amounts of cash spent on food compared to necessities and luxuries. Conversely, the poor household's inability to produce sufficient food for themselves is well demonstrated by their hand-to-mouth economies. Their small expenditure on education (Table 9.5) compared to their large expenditure on necessities and food (Tables 9.7 and 9.8) highlights the dilemma of their poverty. With no cash-generating capacity, households in the poor strata are forced to spend the little cash they can get on 'here and now' basic needs in order to survive. In doing so, they have little to invest in the future; and since most of the households' investment is done through the education of their children, the poor households' relative inability to invest in this way means that their chances of ever escaping from the poverty syndrome are minimized.

How much each stratum contributes to the total expenditure of the sample is shown in Table 9.9.

Table 9.9. Share of Total Expenditure by Stratum

Strata	Amount in K. shillings	Percentage
One	1725.75	17
Two	2100.35	21
Three	2738.15	27
Four	3406.60	34
Total	9970.85	100

Expenditure of the individual strata according to the four categories of items is set out in Table 9.10.

Table 9.10. Expenditure on the Four Categories of Items by Stratum (percentages)

Items	Stratum One	Stratum Two	Stratum Three	Stratum Four
Education	2	26	34	45
Luxuries	7	32	31	27
Necessities	54	20	22	17
Food	37	21	13	11
Total	100	100	100	100

The high expenditure incurred by households for both luxury items and necessities is largely because of the rising prices of these commodities. With their low earning capacity, it is inevitably the poorer households which are hit hardest by these rising prices. And since the production and price-fixing of commodities such as sugar, tea, paraffin, salt and cooking-fat (all necessities) are externally controlled, the peasants have no alternative but to keep purchasing them or do without them altogether. This is one example of how external forces impinge on the rural households' day-to-day way of living. This being a growing process, some of its adverse effects manifest themselves by distorting the eating habits of the peasantry.

Take tea-drinking as an example. Once, tea was taken on social occasions and was hence a luxury, as it still is among the rich. But nowadays it has become a necessity in the sense that it can substitute a meal in the poor households. Ideally, from the peasants' point of view, tea is taken with plenty of milk and sugar. However, the poor households will drink it without milk and sugar (when the tea is known as *kilumbwa*) rather than go completely without. On other occasions, tea is taken with *chakula* as a substitute for *mboga*. Consequently, there is an increasing demand for sugar, and households go to great lengths to get it. Because of their minimal capacity to generate cash earnings, the poor are inevitably obliged to borrow from the rich, thus solidifying the patron/client relationship further by being tied to a web of growing debt relationships.[5]

The functioning of the agricultural cycle is almost totally dependent on the weather. The irrigation system existing is not on a large enough scale to affect the cycle significantly. Hence, with a 4- to 5-month rainy season and a 7- to 8-month hot dry season, each season rapidly giving way to the next, the likelihood of food shortages between harvests becomes real. Food shortage reaches its critical point during the second half of the long rains (see p.29).

This has an obvious bearing on food consumption. I have shown that the sample consumed twelve meals less than its expected potential number of 960 for the 30-day period. These twelve meals were missed by households in the poor strata. Twelve missed meals make a total of 6 days without food. In a year made up of 30-day months, this would mean an average total of 72 days without food for the poor households. These days tend to be lost within the general picture of having enough to eat. However, it would be hard to deny the fact that there exists a kind of hidden starvation which reaches critical proportions about 2 months before the bean harvest.[6] It has been observed that "in the preharvest period, 25 to 30 percent of rural families consume less than 60 percent of estimated calorie requirements" (IBRD Report, 1973). It is precisely at this time that the poor households have to spend much of their cash income on food as well as necessities.

It seems therefore that the move to individual land tenure has not helped to make the poor households self-sufficient in food production. What then has gone wrong? Are there any other alternatives to ameliorate the worsening situation?

---

[5]The debt relationship is to be consolidated further by the Government's proposed "loan programme for stockists of farm inputs (who will) extend credit to those of their customers who are credit worthy" (*Development Plan, 74/78*: 215).

[6]Drought easily uncovers this hidden starvation which then becomes open starvation, as experienced in 1975/76 when the rains failed to come. But there are other symptoms of hidden starvation, the appearance of which and their extent in rural areas are partly due to this phenomenon. Two such symptoms are rural prostitution and petty thieving.

CHAPTER 10

Formal Education: The Parental Gamble and the Growth of a Land Market

In order to understand what has gone wrong, I have attempted to provide a sociological model based on the economic thinking behind the introduction of the individual land-tenure system (see Diagram 10.1).

The central core of the model is the household unit, around which everything revolves. The household is envisaged to operate within first and second levels of 'needs-environment'. However, functioning successfully depends on the household's capacity to operate two basic interactions (each interaction having four permutations) within the first level, which would provide the initial thrust towards the second level, and henceforth to sustained economic growth.

Interaction One: Household $\longrightarrow$ *Shamba*
                   $\uparrow$ $\downarrow$
                   Shamba $\longleftarrow$ Household

Interaction Two: Household $\longrightarrow$ Market
                   $\uparrow$ $\downarrow$
                   Market $\longleftarrow$ Household

The third interaction, household/school, functions as an 'exit' to the second level. Once this second level is reached, the household should be regarded as having the potential to intensify the first two basic interactions and thus attain a high degree of self-sufficiency. However, the previous chapter has shown that the achievement of self-sufficiency is illusory for most poor households. Land reform, with its concomitant maldistribution of land, has opened the 'Pandora's box' of socio-economic differentiation and thus unequally distanced households from fulfilling the conditions laid out in the model. Households in the rich strata are placed in a more advantaged position towards the fulfilment of these conditions than their counterparts in the poor strata (see Diagrams 10.2(a) and 10.2(b)).

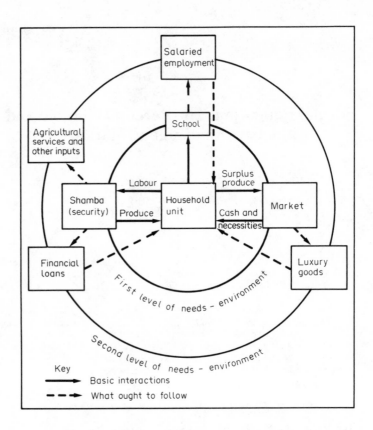

Diagram 10.1.   Model of Envisaged Operation of Land Reform.

With the successful operations of the two basic interactions being more
amenable to rich families than to poor ones, the former have a better chance
of getting into the second level of 'needs-environment' through the third
interaction.   The importance of the third interaction is that both the rich
and poor families regard it as the only 'exit' and that is why they invest
heavily in their children's education (see p.109).   The heavy reliance on
formal education by households is indicative of the malfunctioning of the
model (see Diagram 10.1) and, by implication, the basic tenets of reform.

The Importance of Education

As my analysis of Taita food production and consumption has shown, most
peasants are unable to produce sufficient food supplies for their own needs
in spite of the private ownership of their *shambas*.   It therefore becomes a
logical decision on their part to look for other reliable sources of food
supply.[1]   And even those who are self-sufficient in food production still

---

[1]Meantime, by the end of the 1974/78 Plan period, the Government will have
spent well over 18 million Kenyan pounds on its land-reform programme
(Okoth-Ogendo, 1976).

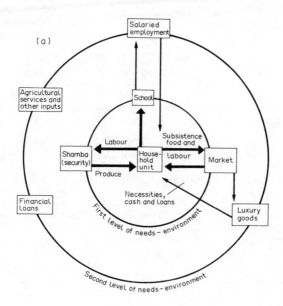

Diagram 10.2(a).   Model of Actual Operation of Land Reform
                   (for poor households).

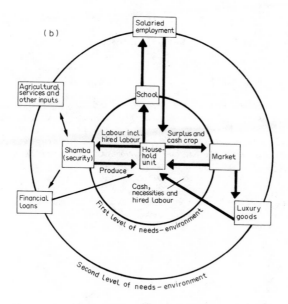

Diagram 10.2(b).   Model of Actual Operation of Land Reform
                   (for rich households).

need non-agricultural skills and income for their economic growth. Hence
the centrality of formal education and the importance of its exit role to
both rich and poor families. In addition, formal education fosters the
belief that the model can be made to function properly if the necessary skill
are acquired.

It is this belief that has made the expenditure-cum-investment in children's
education into a gambling exercise. As such, the odds on winning are stacked
heavily against the poor families, thus committing them to have many children
as their only means of minimizing the chances of losing. The hope is that a
few, or at least one, will make it (Mkangi, 1977).

Invariably, this type of response contributes to the population growth rate
of 3.5 percent a year, which in turn comes into confrontation with a planned
programme like land reform. For example, how will households cope with the
increasing population when they are at present unable to produce sufficient
food for themselves?

I have shown elsewhere (Mkangi, 1977) that the number of children a household
desires is not always prompted by the gambling instinct, but that there is an
inverse correlation between an individual's level of formal education and
the number of children he or she desires (see Table 10.1).

Table 10.1. Educational Level and Desired Number of Children[*]

No. of years of household heads' formal education	No. of respondents	Average no. of children desired
Nil	18	7.6
1 - 4	12	7.0
5 - 8	21	7.1
9 - 12	8	4.6
13 - 14	3	4.0

[*]Source: Mkangi, 1977: 175.

Formal education exposes those who receive it to values and attitudes which
emphasize the importance of having fewer children.[2] This aspect of formal
education is reinforced by a system which in general rewards those who have
had more years of formal education with higher remuneration than those who
have had less years. Indeed, in the above-mentioned article I draw
attention to the fact that there seems to be a "dividing line between those
households with less than £60 *per capita* income and those earning more. . . .
Below this strategic level households have an average of 5.4 children and
their head has an average number of four years of formal education. The
respective figures for the higher income categories are 3.6 children and six
years of formal education . . ." (1977: 176) (see Table 10.2).

---

[2]Also the sheer fact that the educational process is a long one means that
there is a tendency for those who go through it to marry late.

Table 10.2.   Income, Education and Number of Children

Annual per capita income (£ sterling)[+]	Household heads No.	Household heads %		Average no. of children per h/h head[++]		Average no. of years of f/educ. of h/h head	
Below 20	7	19		6.4		3.0	
20 - 39	6	17	66	6.5	5.4	4.5	4.0
40 - 59	11	30		4.6		4.4	
60 - 79	7	19		4.1		4.0	
80 - 99	3	9	34	2.0	3.6	5.5	6.0
100 - 200	2	6		4.5		9.0	

Source: Mkangi, 1977: 177.

[+]The income categories in this column are based on those used in Table 25, ILO Employment Mission Kenya Report, 1975.

[++]There is an uneven age distribution of household heads within the different income categories. Therefore, the difference in the average number of dependent children between households below and above an annual per capita income of £60 cannot be accounted for by the difference in domestic life-cycle phases.

With the level of remuneration pegged to that of formal education and consequently helping to determine fertility patterns, it could be argued that the solution to the population problem lies in the education of the poor peasants. This would be possible if education were free, universal and compulsory;[3] if the economic growth rate kept pace with that of the population;[4] and if school-leavers were assured of gaining employment as they came off the different stages of the educational ladder.

But due to the high-level unemployment it is not just the acquisition of an 'education' which counts if one is to secure a job, but rather the acquisition of a qualificatory education (Dore, 1977; Court and Ghai, 1974).[5] Furthermore, this phenomenon is not a static one; rather, it is dynamic, and there is a tendency to keep upgrading the qualificatory education from time

---

[3]At present formal education is in theory free for the first 7 years of primary education because of a Presidential promulgation of 1979. But in practice parents have to pay more than before the abolition of school fees. Nowadays a child might not be going to school because of non-payment towards either the Building Fund, the Equipment Fund, the Sports Activity Fund, School Uniform or any other 'contribution' that may be demanded by the school committee.

[4]While the population is growing at the rate of 3.5 annually, the actual annual growth of per capita output was 2.6 in 1964/74; and it was targeted to be 4.1 and 2.6 for 1972/78 and 1978/83 Plans respectively (Ministry of Finance, 1977).

[5]With such high unemployment 'tribalism' has in fact sometimes become a more influential deciding factor in the distribution of jobs in the Government and other bureaucracies, than qualificatory education.

to time on the same job and hence also the category of school-leavers.[6] Thus
a job which used to be done satisfactorily by a primary school-leaver 10
years ago is now done by a secondary school-leaver, while that which used to
be done by the latter is now done by a graduate. Thus "10 years ago
'unemployed' primary school leavers were the problem; today it is unemployed
secondary school leavers; very soon it will be unemployed graduates"
(Godfrey and Langdon, 1976: 43).

In response to labour market signals, parents started in the mid-1960s to
take the initiative in building private secondary schools on a *Harambee*
(self-help) basis. For example, between 1967 and 1973, *Harambee* contributed
over 40 percent of the overall national development expenditure on education
and controlled over 62 percent of all secondary schools in the country.
This parental response to labour market signals was easily capitalized by the
politicians to the extent that the '*Harambee* spirit' has now become institu-
tionalized. However, schools founded on a *Harambee* basis do not provide an
easy alternative to Government secondary schools for the poor because of
exorbitant fees, compared to the Government-financed schools. It was partly
to offset this that the National Christian Council of Kenya (NCCK) pioneered
the Village Polytechnic movement. Initially entry to a village polytechnic
was free and was meant to cater for those who had scored the lowest points –
in other words, the failures – in their Certificate of Primary Education
(CPE) examinations. But even here, qualificationism and 'school fees' in
disguised form have set in, thus eliminating many CPE failures, especially
those coming from poor households, from their 'last chance'.[7]

As for the problem of secondary school-leavers, the *Harambee* Institutes of
Technology movement sprung up as a counter-measure in the early 1970s.[8]
This movement operates either at the Provincial or District level; the
ability of either levels to build an institute of technology being largely
determined by the degree of economic and political power it wields at the
centre. In fact, there appears to exist an uncanny relationship between a
Province's level of literacy and the number of institutes it has or plans to
have (see Table 10.3).

The unequal inter-provincial distribution of the institutes is yet another
indicator of the on-going process of socio-economic differentiation.[9] This
process percolates down to the household level, thus rendering opportunities
of formal education to be increasingly determined by the household's socio-
economic status.

Turning to my own sample of a 'dependent' child population numbering 82 only
72 percent (59) actually attend a school; 22 percent (18) are under school-
age and the remaining 6 percent are children who ought to be going to school
but cannot do so because they lack the necessary fees.

---

[6]To make things even more difficult for the school-leaver, there is a
concurrent sharpening of discrimination based on tribal identity, the
definition of a 'tribe' becoming narrower and 'purer'.

[7]For an analysis of this type of examination, which favours children from
rich urban families, see Somerset, 1977.

[8]For a political interpretation of this movement, see Godfrey and Mutiso,
1974.

[9]For recent developments in inter-provincial inequalities, see Bigsten, 1976.

Table 10.3.   Literacy Rate and the Distribution of Institutes
of Technology according to Province

Name of province	Literacy rate % [*]	Number of Institutes
Central	36	4: *Kiambu, Kimathi, Kirinyaga* and *Murang'a.*
Western	32	3: WECO (Western College of Arts and Applied Science) in Kakamega, *Sang'alo* in Bungoma and *Kaimosi* in Wanga.
Nyanza	25	3: RIAT (Ramogi Institute of Advanced Technology) and Gusii; also a technical high school to be built called *Abakuria* THS.
Eastern	24	3: *Embu Karurumo* Polytechnic, *Meru* College of Technology and UKAI (Ukambani Agricultural Institute).
Coast	21	1: CIT (Coast Institute of Technology)
Rift Valley	21	3: RVIST (Rift Valley Institute of Science and Technology), KIAT (Kalenjin Institute of Advanced Technology) and MTS (Maa Technical School).
North-Eastern	3	None.

[*]Source: *Kenya Population Census, 1969,* Vol. III.

Of the school-going cohort of 59, 10 percent (6) are in nursery school, 75 percent (44) are in primary school and 15 percent (9) are in secondary school. School enrolment by these children according to their socio-economic strata is given in Table 10.4.

Table 10.4.   School-going Children by Stratum

Strata	% of sample	Nursery No.	%	Primary No.	%	Secondary No.	%	Total No.	%
One	28	–	–	12	27	–	–	12	20
Two	21	–	–	6	14	3	33	9	15
Three	31	3	50	20	45	2	22	25	43
Four	20	3	50	6	14	4	45	13	22
Total		6	100	44	100	9	100	59	100

The small proportion who go to nursery school is explained by the fact that it is not necessary for a child to go to nursery school before it proceeds to primary school. As a result, the poor peasants who are unable to afford the 'small money contribution' necessary for admittance to a nursery school, usually make their children skip this stage, thus putting them in a disadvantaged position when they are eventually enrolled at the primary level. Parents try their best to send their children to primary school at least, and this partially accounts for the five-fold increase in attendance at this stage. Enrolment at secondary school is dependent on passing the CPE examination. The sifting which this examination is supposed to perform explains the elimination of two-thirds of the number of primary school children from secondary education.

Table 10.4 shows the influence of socio-economic variables in determining children's exposure to formal education. This influence is most pronounced at the secondary level where children from Stratum Four, in spite of making up just under a quarter of the dependent child population, account for 45 percent of the places. As a whole, the rich strata account for almost two-thirds of the secondary-school places. The poor strata account for the remaining one-third, with the poorest accounting for none. But of the three children involved from the poor strata, two are in a *Harambee* school where they might be forced to drop out because of the comparatively expensive school fees. The remaining child is in a Government-subsidized secondary school, helped through the educational system by bursaries from the local County Council.

It is this small percentage attending the Government secondary schools who provide the basis for optimistic parental gambling, in terms of their chance of breaking through the poverty syndrome in which they are caught. Even here, the chances are reduced to a near impossibility, statistically speaking due to the hierarchical grading of Government secondary schools. The schools are graded according to the Government's financial commitment to them. Those schools designated as 'national' ones - e.g. Alliance High School (Central Province), Mangu High School (Eastern Province), Shimo-la-Tewa High School (Coast Province) - are qualitatively superior to other Government secondary schools. Whatever the optimism poorer households have towards formal education, the chances for a successful breakthrough are, for the majority, very slim indeed. However, this has not (as yet) diminished the poor peasants' faith in seeing education as their economic salvation in spite of the unemployment problem facing secondary school-leavers. Like true gamblers, the hope of winning against all the odds prompts them finally to throw in their trump card. For the poor peasants, this card is their private land, and it is this that they will sooner or later be forced to surrender.

The Creation of a Land Market

Changing a communal land-tenure system into a freehold tenure system transforms land into a negotiable asset which can be rented, pawned, bought, sold, mortgaged, etc. This is one of the main reasons behind the implementation of the reform and is the most easily achievable.[10]

Of course there was selling and buying of land in pre-reform days (see p.30) but not on the same scale and with the same thrust. The reform has speeded up the maturation of this nascent process by removing the communalistic ethos which was keeping in check the growth towards individual land tenure. The introduction of individual land tenure has automatically ushered in the creation of a land market where land transaction is on a willing-seller willing-buyer basis. It is the existence of this land market which offers the poor peasants an alternative means of raising the cash needed to educate

---

[10]See IBRD, 1973: Annex 3:10.

their children - although of course cash raised through the selling of land
is not always for this purpose. It is an alternative which, if resorted to,
is more likely to exacerbate rather than ameliorate the abject conditions
in which the poor peasants are caught.

Market forces have already begun to operate in Shigaro-Sungululu Sub-location.
With the whole Sub-location mapped into twelve units of consolidated and
registered land plots (see Appendix V), the process of land transaction
operates between and within these units.

On checking the land record, the picture that emerges is that on the whole
each registered unit has either gained or lost some land.[11] A unit gains
some land if the acreage of land sold from it is less than the acreage of
land bought from 'outside'. I term this *positive transaction*. Conversely,
when a unit's total acreage sold is more than that bought, I term this
negative transaction. Of the twelve registered units, six recorded positive
and the other six negative transactions (see Table 10.5).

Table 10.5. Positive (Purchase) and Negative (Sale) Land Transactions
in Shigaro-Sungululu by Plot Sub-location (1969*-1975)

Plot No.	Total acres	Positive transaction (purchases in acres)	Negative transactions (sales in acres)	Average landholding per household in acres	
				1969	1975
263	48.20	-	11.5	1.42	1.32
264	147.35	30.6	-	1.50	1.71
286	136.76	-	40.3	1.95	1.71
287	414.17	130.41	-	1.58	1.66
288	103.62	-	27.5	1.46	1.28
310	237.90	54.4	-	1.98	2.12
311	179.30	-	63.1	1.91	1.84
333	159.91	21.9	-	1.26	1.32
334	151.04	-	20.1	1.08	0.99
356	17.20	3.8	-	1.72	1.73
357	31.10	-	6.6	1.94	1.74
309	13.56	2.16	-	4.52	5.42

*1969 is the year the reform was first introduced in Taita-Taveta District.

The extent of differentiation is magnified by looking at the transformation
in the size of the biggest and smallest *shambas* within a given registered
unit after a negative and positive transaction, as shown in Table 10.6.
This highlights the on-going process of differentiation. The widening of
the gap is happening in the most classical way, with those owning the bigger
shambas selling relatively little, but accumulating small pieces of land
from here and there. An examination of the smallest *shamba* on either side
of the transaction illuminates this process. For example, on the sales side
the smallest *shambas* have on average decreased in size by 9 percent, while on
the purchase side they have increased by 141 percent. This contrast
encapsulates the process of the creation of landlessness in the rural

---

[11]To show how the market forces operate, I am examining here the whole
Sub-location within which my small sample is scattered.

areas.[12] The virtual 'disappearance' of the smallest *shamba* in Plot no. 288
(Table 10.6) on the sales side portends the intensification of this process.

Table 10.6. The Widening of the Gap between Big and Small Shambas
within Individual Consolidated Plots (1969-1975)

Land transactions (1969-1975)								
Negative (sales)				Positive (purchases)				
Average landholding per biggest *shamba*		Average landholding per smallest *shamba*		Average landholding per biggest *shamba*		Average landholding per smallest *shamba*		
Plot No.	Before	After	Before	After	Plot No.	Before	After	Before	After
	acres	acres	acres	acres		acres	acres	acres	acres
263	4.20	4.03	0.20	0.19	264	6.00	6.84	0.10	0.11
286	9.70	9.38	0.20	0.17	287	11.10	11.77	0.10	0.11
288	11.10	8.33	0.01	0.009	310	13.60	14.56	0.10	0.11
311	11.10	10.66	0.20	0.19	333	5.20	5.62	0.10	0.11
334	4.50	4.14	0.20	0.18	356	3.40	3.42	0.70	0.70
357	4.50	4.05	0.60	0.54	309	8.70	10.44	2.00	2.44

The emergence of landlessness was foreseen by the chief architect of the land
reform, Swynnerton, who nevertheless regarded the emergence of this
phenomenon together with its attendant problems as "a normal and necessary
step in the evolution of a country". While the acceleration of buying and
selling land has been precipitated by the reform, the emergence of a landless
peasantry has also been hastened by the intensification of the exploitative
forces released by it, and which in turn have unleashed the paradoxical
distortion in the rate of population growth and the need for the continuation
of a customary law of inheritance.

With population increasing at an annual rate of 3.5 percent and an inheritance law which is through the male line only but recognizes no primogeni-
ture, the interplay of these variables inevitably leads to a rapid diminution
of the consolidated holding. With the poor households having the smallest
holdings, population growth and the division of these holdings through
inheritance is succeeding in fragmenting them to such sub-economic units
that, if they are to be turned back to viable agricultural production, they
will need to be re-consolidated. Re-consolidation can be achieved by either

---

[12]Previously, the Government had created Land Control Boards whose main
objective was to see that any land transaction would not lead to landlessness. But since these Boards are hindering the establishment of "an
active land market . . . Land Control Boards will be asked to encourage the
subdivision of land holdings . . ." (*Development Plan, 1974/8*: 199).

the rich buying the poor out[13] or the Government one day passing a
're-consolidation land reform' act! Whatever the option taken, it looks as
if the future can only lead to further consolidation - not to the
eradication of poverty. It is against this background that the introduction
of an ameliorative programme such as family planning should be examined.

---

[13]A verbal communication from Professor Steppler of the Faculty of
  Agriculture, University of Montreal, Canada, confirms my observation. He
  told me that in Quebec Province, where farms tend to end at the river-
  banks, subdivision through inheritance has produced very narrow sub-
  economic strips of land stretching back from the river-banks, thus making
  re-consolidation a prerequisite to the creation of viable economic
  holdings. This is done by the rich buying out their poorer neighbours.

CHAPTER 11

Family Planning: The Wish, the Knowledge and the Practice

According to the Development Plan, "the basic reason for unemployment is the rapid growth in population. Not only has the population itself been growing, but so also has the rate of annual increase - from 3.2 percent between 1948 and 1962 to approximately 3.5 percent today" (1974/78: 99). To solve the problem of population growth which together with others, such as poverty and income distribution, "are deeply embedded in the economic and social structure" (Plan, 1974/8: 90) the Government has developed a strategy which has six basic elements: Continued Rapid Economic Growth, Family Planning, Income Redistribution, Agricultural and Rural Modernization, Education Reform and the Promotion of Small-scale Enterprises (Plan, 1974/8: 91).

With Family Planning rated very highly, one would like to know the constraints which prevent it being widely adopted by the peasants, and also the common characteristics which exist among those who avail themselves of the facilities offered by the programme.

In an attempt to answer these two questions, I collected two sorts of data - primary and secondary. The primary data involved using a questionnaire entitled *Case Histories of Child-bearing Women*, which was administered to women who were actually pregnant at the time. The women were interviewed at maternity clinics after they had been examined by the midwife. The data was collected under five major categories: age/marital status, education, religion, childbirth histories and attitudes as well as perception.

The secondary data involved working through family planning records available for the period from June 1975 to June 1976. The aim was to find out the common characteristics of the family planning clients, especially those who either had used or were at the time using contraceptives.

Pregnant Women

The primary data collected reveals that of the total fifty-one respondents, all were married except three, two of whom were already unmarried mothers; their age distribution is shown in Table 11.1.

Table 11.1. Respondents' Distribution by Age Cohorts

Age cohort	No. of respondents	Percentage
15-19	10	20
20-24	14	27
25-29	15	29
30-34	3	6
35-39	7	14
40+	2	4
Total	51	100

Table 11.2 shows the educational attainment of the respondents.

Table 11.2. Respondents' Levels of Education

Level of education	No. of respondents	Percentage
No formal education	18	35
1-4 yr (Lower Primary)	12	24
5-8 yr (Upper Primary)	18	35
9-10yr (Junior Secondary)	2	4
11-12yr ('O' Level)	1	2
Total	51	100

The women interviewed belonged to two religious denominations - they were either Catholics or Protestants (see Table 11.3). The latter have three main segments in Taita. The 'nominal' wing composed of self-professed churchgoing Christians. Secondly, the 'saved' wing, whose devotees are practising Christians. Both the 'nominal' and 'saved' wings belong to one Church, namely the Church of the Province of Kenya (CPK), which is the new name for the Anglican Church Missionary Society (CMS) sect. Finally, the 'Gospel' wing, whose followers are fanatical/revivalist type of Christians. This wing exists as a separate church and, in general, it attracts those living in anomie-prone conditions. Poverty and 'being a woman' seem to be the dominant characteristics in such conditions, hence the majority of the adherents are poor and, frequently, post-menopausal women.

Table 11.3. Respondents' Distribution According to Religious Faiths

Religion	No. of respondents	Percentage
Catholic	20	39
Nominal Wing - CPK	24	47
Saved Wing - CPK	3	6
Gospel	4	8
Total	51	100

The followers of the CPK 'Saved' and 'Gospel' wing have much in common as regards their faiths. As such, their world outlook seems to be the same, especially in matters concerning contraception. Though forming only 14 percent of the total their influence is greater than their number warrants because of the social position they tend to hold in the household.

Child-birth histories of respondents were collected by asking first the number of pregnancies (conceptions) ever had inclusive of the current one. The question put was: "What nth pregnancy is this?"

Out of the total 246 pregnancies, eleven had ended in miscarriage or still-born births (see Table 11.4). Of those women involved, nine had had the experience once and one had had it twice. In other words, 20 percent of the respondents had had miscarriages or pregnancies ending in still-born births.

Table 11.4.   Fertility Histories of Respondents

nth no. of current pregnancy	Respondents		Total no. of pregnancies ever conceived		No. of miscarriages and still-births	
	no.	$\%^*$	no.	$\%^{**}$	no.	$\%^{***}$
1st	7	13	7	2.8	–	–
2nd	9	18	19	7.7	1	9
3rd	6	12	20	8.0	2	18
4th	7	13	31	12.6	3	27
5th	5	10	25	10.2	–	–
6th	6	12	36	14.6	–	–
7th	4	8	28	11.4	–	–
9th	1	2	9	3.7	–	–
10th	6	12	71	29.0	5	46
Total	51	100	246	100	11	100

*The percentage is out of a total of 51 respondents.
**The percentage is out of a total of 246 pregnancies ever conceived.
***The percentage is out of a total of 11 miscarriages/still-births.

Having given the nth number of their pregnancies, respondents were asked to state the number of their living children and their sexes. Table 11.5 sets out the answers of the 42 respondents who at the time had a child or children living.

Of the children alive at the time, 66 (42.6 percent) are sons and 89 (54.4 percent) are daughters. And of the 42 mothers, 34 (81 percent) each have a son or more than 1 son living, while 36 (86 percent) each have a daughter or more than 1 daughter living. The distribution of sons and daughters per mother is shown in Tables 11.6 and 11.7.

Table 11.5.   Total Number of Live Births in Relation to the
              Total Number of Living Children per Woman

nth no. of children living	Respondents		Total no. of live births		Total no. of living children	
	no.	%*	no.	%**	no.	%***
1	10	24	12	6.7	10	6.4
2	5	12	10	5.6	10	6.4
3	7	17	27	15.0	21	13.5
4	5	12	21	11.7	20	13.0
5	7	17	42	23.1	35	22.6
6	1	2	6	3.3	6	4.0
7	3	7	28	15.6	21	13.5
8	4	9	34	19.0	32	20.6
Total	42	100.0	180	100.0	155	100.0

*The percentage is out of a total of 42 mothers.
**The percentage is out of a total of 180 live births.
***The percentage is out of a total of 155 living children.

Table 11.6.   Number of Living Sons per Woman

nth no. of living sons	Respondents		Total no. of living sons	
	no.	%	no.	%
1	14	41.0	14	21.2
2	11	32.0	22	33.3
3	6	18.0	18	27.3
4	3	9.0	12	18.2
Total	34	100.0	66	100.0

Table 11.7.   Number of Living Daughters per Woman

nth no. of living daughters	Respondents		Total no. of living daughters	
	no.	%	no.	%
1	12	33.0	12	13.5
2	8	22.0	16	18.0
3	6	17.0	18	20.2
4	7	20.0	28	31.5
5	3	8.0	15	16.8
Total	36	100.0	89	100.0

A total of 16 (31 percent) respondents had already lost 1 child or more. Of these 16, 10 had lost altogether 15 male children. Of these 10 mothers, 7 had each lost 1 son, 1 had lost 2 sons and 2 had each lost 3 sons. In other words, 20 percent of the total sample had lost on average 1.5 sons each.

The remaining 6 (out of the 16 respondents who had lost a child or children) had altogether lost a total of 10 female children. Four mothers had each lost a daughter; and 2 had each lost 3 daughters. In other words, 12 percent of the total sample had lost on average 1.7 daughters each.

The total number of children born alive but now dead was 25 (14 percent of the total number of children born alive), which means that the 51 mothers in the sample had lost on average 0.5 of a child each.[1] Most of the 25 children had died before reaching the age of 5. To elicit attitudinal and/or perceptual response from the respondents they were asked about their feelings towards their pregnancy. Were they happy or sad, did they feel it was routine or did they have a sense of loss? (see Table 11.8).

Table 11.8.   Respondents Feelings Towards their Pregnancies

Nature of response	No. of respondents	Percentage
Happy	30	59
Routine	13	25
Sad	5	10
Loss	3	6
Total	51	100.0

There is nothing very spectacular about pregnant women feeling happy or routine towards their pregnancies. The 43 (84 percent) who felt either happy or routine may have done so for many and varied reasons. However, most of them answered spontaneously, so that their responses can be seen as the stereotype ones to be expected from women in such conditions, whatever

[1]For the impact of death on fertility, see the concluding chapter.

the underlying reasons behind such responses. Or they may have given the
answers they felt were expected of them.

It is quite the opposite, however, when it comes to the 8 women (16 percent)
who felt sadness or loss towards their pregnancies. The majority of them
were young (15-24 years) and/or single. Those over 24 years felt no sense
of loss but rather saddened by the little 'breathing-space' between the birth
of their last child and conception. "I am sad because I did not expect it
so soon after giving birth" was so often the lament.

As for those who felt a sense of loss, a common characteristic running
through is their educational level. They had all more than the primary level
of formal education and the one who felt the most loss was a 19-year-old
unmarried girl who had gone as far as doing her 'O' levels.

Each respondent was also asked whether she had hoped to fall pregnant.
Thirty-two (63 percent) answered in the positive; the rest in the negative.
The 8 respondents who were saddened or felt a sense of loss confirmed their
feelings by answering "No". In addition, 10 of those who had regarded
their pregnancies as routine and one who felt happy over hers, also joined
the 8 by saying that their pregnancies were unexpected.

When asked "Would you like God to protect you from falling pregnant again?",
55 percent said "Yes", the rest answered negatively.

While the majority declared their wish to have God intervene with their
fertility, nevertheless the un-Godliness inherent in such a wish to which
the minority reacted against is portrayed in the answers given by the CPK
'Saved' and 'Gospel' Wing followers. It is these two sects whose 'No'
responses outnumber their 'Yes' ones, thus confirming the belief they hold
that everything that happens to them is ordained by God - and "He knows
best".

Enquiries relating to knowledge of any traditional or modern method of
contraception showed that twenty-eight (55 percent) of the respondents knew
some contraceptive method. Here too the percentage distribution of the
positive and negative answers according to religious beliefs illustrates the
correlation between religious beliefs and attitude towards family planning:
among the CPK 'Saved' and 'Gospel' Wing followers the negative responses by
far outweigh the positive ones; for the rest the reverse holds true.
Educational level is another vehicle which affects contraceptive knowledge.
The impact of formal education seems to separate those who have had 4 years
or less from those who have had more than 4 years. Those respondents who
have had 4 or less years of formal education or none at all are equally
divided between the 'Yes' and 'No' responses. As for those who have had 5
or more years of formal education, it is interesting to note that, though
a minority (41 percent of the sample), a higher percentage of them (62 percent) have responded positively.

The respondents with 0-4 years of formal education who answered that they
knew some contraceptive method might have done so due to a multiplicity of
factors such as age, number of living children, urbanity, religion, husband/
wife relationship, and so on.

When asked whether they ever used any contraceptive method only four (8 percent) answered in the positive; they had used modern methods, the Pill in
particular. The gap existing between the *Wish*, the *Knowledge* and the
Practice is well illustrated by the fact that while 55 percent of the total

sample responded positively to the questions relating to desire for and knowledge of family planning only 8 percent had actually used contraceptives.[2]
As for these users, despite individual characteristics, the deciding factor
tended to be the sanction of the husband.[3] This is borne out in the response
to the question. "Could you use contraceptives without your husband's
consent?" Here too only 4 respondents answered in the affirmative. But only
one of them belongs to the initial 4 respondents of the previous question,
this makes her an intriguing character indeed. It is difficult to understand
how she could use contraceptives without her husband's consent. She has
many attributes which are associated with subservience to a husband: she is
middle-aged (36), has had no formal education and has no employment; she is
a Gospel Wing follower and has 5 living children - 4 daughters and a son.
Could it be something to do with her strong character and what is chauvin-
istically regarded as 'feminine guile'? For in addition to her other
attributes, she is quite urbanized in her way of life. It could be true that
she would use contraceptives without her husband's consent. She also told
me that she has a 5-year *natural* spacing period between her children. In
other words, it apparently takes her 5 years after giving birth to experience
her menstruation cycle again!

As for the remaining three who said that they can use contraceptive devices
without their husband's knowing, the youngest two (19 and 22 years) are both
unmarried. Blaming men for their condition, it is quite probable that they
express their 'men-hating' attitudes by assuming that they would use
contraceptives without their husbands' consent if they were married.

The last one is a 23-year-old married mother. She has the attributes which
would enable her to practice contraception even with her husband's
disapproval. She is a trained and employed teacher and a nominal CPK
Christian.

Her case epitomizes the only way for a woman who would like to practise
contraception but is forbidden to do so by her husband: a good education,
good permanent employment and the 'liberation' that this gives her. But it
is an uphill struggle for women to achieve this goal because of the socio-
economic and cultural hurdles they have to overcome. And, as shown in
Chapters 2 and 8, these hurdles are deeply embedded in the intra-household
arrangements.

Contraceptive Users

From June 1975 to June 1976, family planning clinics in Taita Hills dealt
with 144 clients, all of them women (see Table 11.9).

---

[2]This gap does not exist only for women in a developing country like Kenya.
It is also found to exist among women in a developed country such as
England (see Peel and Carr, 1975: 63-72).

[3]Many women would not use contraceptives even if their husbands consented,
on religious and maternal grounds. This is how a 32-year-old wife and
mother of six, expecting her seventh child, put it: "Even if he allowed me
to use them, I would however not use them at all. It is God who gives me
children. I am just His instrument for bringing them forth into the world.
Therefore I refuse to do God's work." Thus she would not like to interfere
with her fertility.

Table 11.9. Age Distribution of Women who use
            Contraceptives

Age cohort	No. of respondents	Percentage
15-19	18	12
20-24	63	44
25-29	32	22
30-34	16	11
35-39	11	8
40-44	4	3
Total	144	100

With the twenty to twenty-four cohort providing almost half the total number
of contraceptive users, and with nearly 80 percent of them under 30 years,
it is possible that the majority of them use contraceptives more for child
spacing rather than fertility control. The marital status of the respondents
could throw some light on this (Table 11.10).

Table 11.10. Marital Status of Contraceptive Users

Marital status	No. of respondents	Percentage
Married	90	62.5
Single	43	29.9
Divorced	11	7.6
Total	144	100

Those users above 30 years normally resort to contraceptives as a terminal
measure, that is, after they have had the number of children they desire. On
average, this is over five children. This terminal use of contraceptives is
especially the case where single and divorced women are concerned. These
make up 26 percent of the over-30s, thus making their contribution to
fertility control more significant.

The total of 144 women have between them 465 living children. The mothers
under 30 years have between them 303 (65 percent of the total) children,
while those over 30 years have between them 162 (35 percent) children. Hence,
on average those under 30 have 2.7 children, while those over have 5.2
children.

The educational level of the contraceptive users is relatively high,
especially when compared to that of the 51 pregnant women who were the source
of the primary data (see Table 11.2). At one end of the scale, 35 percent of
the pregnant women have had no formal education, while only 22 percent of the
contraceptive users have had none (see Table 11.11). At the other end of the
scale, only 2 percent of the pregnant women and as many as 10 percent of the
contraceptive users have had 11-12 years or more of formal education.

Table 11.11. Educational Level of Contraceptive Users

Educational level	No. of respondents	Percentage
No formal education	32	22
1-4 years	36	25
5-8 years	55	38
9-10 years	7	5
11-12+ years	14	10

Married women make up almost two-thirds of the users, and it can be assumed that the majority of them are using contraceptives for spacing rather than fertility control. On the other hand, it is likely that the single women and divorcees, who in all make up over one-third of the users, are taking birth-preventative measures to control their fertility rather than to space births. The introduction of the age variable might help to clarify these phenomena.

Table 11.12 indicates that of those women under 30 years (i.e. 113) 67 were married, 39 single and 7 divorced. With more than half of the under-30s married, it is likely that the effect of contraceptives on their fertility will be very slight, especially since they are largely dominated by their husbands and relatives who favour large families.

Table 11.12. Contraceptive Users according to Marital Status and Age

Age cohort	Marital status					
	Married		Single		Divorced	
	no.	%	no.	%	no.	%
15-19	11	7.6	6	4.2	1	0.7
20-24	38	26.4	21	14.6	4	2.7
25-29	18	12.5	12	8.3	2	1.4
30-34	11	7.6	3	2.1	2	1.4
35-39	8	5.6	1	0.7	2	1.4
40-44	4	2.8	-	-	-	-
Total	90	62.5	43	29.9	11	7.6

It is the interaction of formal education, age and marital status which determines the propensity for using contraceptives. For example, taking the education and marital status variables, one sees that there tends to be more illiteracy among the married contraceptive users than among the single and divorced. The illiteracy rates for the married, single and divorced users are 25.5 percent, 16.3 percent and 18.2 percent respectively. Bringing in the age variable, irrespective of their marital status, women below 30 years have an illiteracy rate of 19.5 percent as compared to 32.3 percent for those over 30 years. Indeed, with the exception of one, none of the women over 30 years has had more than 8 years of formal education.

Poverty and Family Planning

A common feature emerging out of this data is that contraception methods appeal to a large spectrum of the female population in the rural areas. There is, however, an ambivalence as regards the ultimate aim of Family Planning policy on the part of those responsible for its implementation. Is the policy's ultimate goal to achieve a reduction in the rate of population growth? Or is it simply to offer better spacing facilities?

The primary data quoted here indicates that the novelty of marriage and children and the need to prove one's fertility starts to wane after the fourth or fifth pregnancy, or after having four living children. For most women the actual continuation of child-bearing is not questioned. This is so firstly because of the inability to determine the sex composition of their children and the risk of losing a child.[4] Secondly, women tend not to question whether or not they should have more children because of their socio-cultural and economic environment (see Chapters 2 and 8).

True this environment can be tampered with and become less suffocating by the introduction of a variable such as formal education. The interaction of formal education and age makes women more amenable to contraception. However, this interaction is not easy to achieve due to a multiplicity of intervening factors.

The desire for many children - five or more, with at least two sons - is socio-culturally determined. But I have also shown that children are a prerequisite to the economic upkeep of the household. Paradoxically despite improved health conditions, a falling infant mortality rate and individualized landholdings, parents still see in a large family the potential for improving their economic condition (Peet and White, 1977: 123-140 and 141-156). This is because of the peculiar relationship which exists between poverty and family size.

Poverty is the core problem, and within this framework children are seen both as social wealth in themselves (Mkangi, 1977: 178-9) and as economic assets (Mkangi, 1975: 60-64).[5] It is basically this last role ascribed to children which concretizes the reasons for having them beyond the usual psycho-socio-cultural legitimation. The ability to strip off this legitimizing ideology depends on creating the socio-economic conditions which will dysfunctionalize children. However, the dysfunctionalization of children will be hard to achieve as long as poverty continues to exist or policies are embarked upon, such as land reform, which end up by aggravating the situation.

---

[4] In a society where male children have higher status than female ones, the phase during her fertility period when a woman gives birth to a son or sons becomes important. The longer it takes her, the less amenable she would be to contraception.

[5] Peet and White observe that "While the emotional rewards of having children may be assumed to provide one of the main motivations for parents in both industrialized and peasant societies, the economic value of children may be assumed to provide an important motivation for parents in peasant societies" (1977: 124).

Indeed, by a subtle twist of logic, the implementation of an individual
tenure system has produced certain side-effects which have re-emphasized the
'conservative' values and attitudes of the socio-cultural milieu which go to
justify the necessity of having a large family. For what the reform has
done to the majority of the peasants is to make them more aware of how small
their *shambas* are and thus bring home to them their inability to make ends
meet. This forces them to depend less on their land and more on their
children - and the more the better. And as I have shown in Chapters 8 and
10 the sheer economic existence of a household depends very much on the
number of children it has at its disposal.

Hence, the introduction of the Family Planning programme should be regarded
as a stop-gap measure for the population as a whole rather than for the
individual household. For while my data shows the existence of potential
widespread use of contraceptives, I am unable to foresee any significant
fertility decline, nor any improvement in the levels of living among the
many poor Taita, bearing in mind the external forces impinging on them.
It is these forces which paradoxically create the poor households' practical
solution (i.e. large families) to the poverty syndrome in which they find
themselves locked![6]

---

[6] See Epstein and Jackson, 1975.

CHAPTER 12

Conclusion

This final chapter attempts to synthesise the preceding argument by analysing the implications of applying "Western-based Development Models" to Third World countries like Kenya. I focus here on the institution of individualistic private property and the small family norm which are two of the most important integral parts of industrial capitalist countries. In doing so I try to examine the social cost involved when developing societies, like the Taita, change from being community-centred and kin-oriented to becoming individualistically-based with small nuclear families.

Why Private Ownership of Land?

The idea behind the implementation of tenure reform throughout the country is to encourage the growth of a private-property mentality in the people, even if many of them will be denied the capacity to own a plot. This is the primary goal of the reform, contrary to the stated goal which is ". . . to redress the imbalance in landholding so that production from all areas can be expanded" (IBRD, 1973: 10). It is advice of this kind, coming from experts, which gives the reform its *raison d'être*, and encourages the Government to continue to lay ". . . emphasis on the acceleration of land adjudication and registration" (*Development Plan, 1974/78:* 59). This is in spite of the fact that many studies (Wasserman, 1973; Leys, 1975; Okoth-Ogendo, 1976, etc.) have come to the following conclusion:

> ". . . [while] the land reform in the African areas has been a major change, *it would be wrong to see it as the fundamental cause of progress in small-scale agriculture* . . . [for example] the Agricultural Finance Corporation (AFC) provides credit to virtually all large-scale farmers but to little more than one percent of small farmers. . . . *It would not be universally accepted that the increase in African participation and African money income in the aggregate is sufficient evidence on which to pronounce the policy towards agriculture and land tenure a success*" (Holtham and Hazlewood, 1976: 23; emphasis added).

135

The Government's continued implementation of land reform becomes hard to understand when even its own appointed mission on land consolidation and registration reported the following as early as 1965/66:

> "The Government is not only attempting a task of unparalleled magnitude but could in many places be merely *handing a stone to the man who is asking for bread.*
>
> The criticism that consolidation initially creates unemployment and landlessness is a valid one.
>
> The benefits of enclosure to arable farming are less obvious. . . ." (Verhelst, 1968: 418-419; emphasis added).

That the Government is handing a stone to the man who is asking for bread, in spite of his owning a holding, comes out clearly when it is remembered that most of the peasants are unable to produce enough food supplies on their *shambas* even for their own domestic consumption (see Chapter 9). Why, then, is land reform still pursued vigorously by the Government in its endeavours to develop the country?

Leys says that it has to do so because the country is heavily tied to external forces and it is they who lend the Government the money to implement the policy. Moreover, their major objective is not to make the peasants self-sufficient in food production (although if some of them manage to become so, then well and good); but rather, they aim

> ". . . *to break down precapitalist attitudes and social institutions* and replace them with the ideas of incentives of the market.
>
> The *inner secret* of the drive towards complete individual freehold land tenure was thus not so much its particular merits as its general merits; it flowed logically from the critical decision to accept the general structure of colonial economy. That structure rested on individual property . . . and land was the main asset of the Africans . . ." (Leys, *op.cit.*: 72; emphasis added).

It is not difficult, therefore, to see the direct and logical correlation between land reform and the inevitably resulting values and attitudes which justify limitless ownership of property by individuals;[1] the same values and attitudes also justify family planning and the emergence of the small nuclear family institution.

When it comes to the 'Third World', social scientists from the 'developed' countries have either ignored or laid little emphasis on the dangers accruing from the development of private property with its attendant materialism. Rarely have these social scientists stopped in their tracks to look at the pace of disintegration of their own societies, let alone attribute most of it to the capitalistic mode of production existing in their countries. Instead, there is a sense of self-righteousness which assumes that whatever

---

[1] A point at hand here is that up to now the Government has shown no intention of establishing a land ceiling; on the contrary, it has opposed any attempts to establish such a ceiling. The extent of this opposition comes out clearly when an Assistant Minister of Lands and Settlement distorts Para. 106 of Sessional Paper No. 10 - *African Socialism and its Application to Planning in Kenya* (1965) - by claiming that it allows for non-ceiling of land-ownership (*The National Assembly Official Report*, 1973: 632-33).

has happened in the industrialized countries must surely be good for the
non-industrialized countries too. Hence neither they nor their benefactors
stop to question the fundamental validity behind their endeavours to
construct a development strategy for the non-industrialized countries from
which, up to now, only a minority have benefited, both within the countries
concerned as well as outside.

It is no secret that the privileged minority in the Third World countries
are in league with the powerful minorities of the developed countries. As
such, the political survival of this internal minority is very much
dependent on the continued support from their external counterparts, in the
form of both financial and military aid.[2] Also, the perpetuation of this
link is reinforced by the propagation of a multinational value system.
This value system emanates from the developed countries and is imparted to
the privileged minority in the developing countries through the former's
educational system. This is what the Deputy Administrator of USAID,
Mr. Coffin, has to say concerning the activities of his Agency in the
educational field:

> "The Agency annually brings to the United States 6000 foreign nationals
> for study and training in technical and professional fields . . . their
> training is directly related to development objectives in their home
> countries. . . . They return to their homes to add not only increased
> skill and competence, but *whatever they have absorbed of the values of
> our society.* . . . The opportunity for *broad social and political
> orientation* exists at every point in the total experience the participant
> has while in the United States . . ." (George, 1976: 70; emphasis added).

Furthermore, the intentions behind such training schemes are not primarily
to serve the interests of the developing countries, as Mr. Coffin makes quite
clear:

> *"Our basic, broadest goal is a long range political one.* It is not
> development for the sake of sheer development. . . . An important
> objective is to open up the maximum opportunity for domestic private
> initiative and to insure that foreign private investment, particularly
> from the United States, is welcomed and well treated . . ." (George,
> 1976: 71; emphasis added).

To recapitulate, one is driven to question the validity of the use by social
scientists of developed countries as models of economic development, whose
basis lies in the ownership of private property. The cost of following
such development strategy is clearly summed up by Sunkel:

> "Two decades of unprecedented growth in the capitalist economy has in
> fact also had some unanticipated effects on the industrial countries
> themselves, giving rise to strong internal criticism: alienation,
> consumerism, waste, concentration of power, destruction of the environ-
> ment, bureaucratisation, the loss of jobs . . ., etc., are all the
> phenomena which contribute to cast serious doubt on whether the so-called
> developed countries really are the ideal model of development that they
> were supposed to be" (1976: 17).

---

[2]Barnaby says that "about two-thirds of the current global arms trade is to
the Third World Countries", (Jolly, 1978: 15).

In Kenya, private property as introduced through land reform is the most
significant means through which the country is attempting to model its
development on the lines of the developed countries.

But already there are signs of disintegration at work, as can be witnessed
in a community like Taita. Here, the process of nucleation of the family
and residential patterns seems to have reached an irreversible stage.
Extended family villages have been broken up and people are now settled in
individualized homesteads *cum shambas*, separated from one another by petty
fencing or shrub boundaries. This environment provides the appropriate
atmosphere for incessant squabbles among neighbours. These squabbles, which
range from shouting matches, witchcraft accusations to physical assaults,
can be triggered off by a straying chicken, cow or goat, or even by grass
growing across the great divide, or boundaries.[3] Such manifestations of
tension contribute further to the breakdown of the social fabric of the
community's life.[4] In the transition from community to individuals the total
disappearance of an institution such as the *kichuku*, as well as the communal
ethos of the people, becomes logical (see Chapter 2).

The goal of the development strategy is to cater for the individual; but at
the same time it cannot be said that in its efforts to develop the country
the Government is specifically aiming at the disintegration of the different
communities and community life in general. As such, would this not be the
right time to question the current model of development? As one Kenyan
proverb advises: "If you see a hyena eating a dying person, you the healthy
one close the door." The country can start closing the door by stopping
further implementation of the land-tenure reform right now. By so doing, it
may be possible to examine the 'population problem' within its proper
perspective.

Why a Small Family?

I am not questioning here the sheer 'economic' advantages of having a small
family - if indeed there are any. Instead I am looking at the less explored
'dark side' of the small family norm in industrialized society.

So far, the implementation of family planning in most developing countries has
gone largely unquestioned because of the belief that together with other
measures, such as land reform, it will eventually bring about economic
development. I hope I have shown in Chapter 10 that this belief is mis-
guided. But for the sake of argument, supposing that this belief were well-
founded, one has to ask what cost does the country have to pay within the
existing socio-economic structure, for the changes in family size brought
about by a successful family planning programme directed towards economic
development?

---

[3]One day the Sub-Chief of Werugha invited me to attend a meeting to solve a
boundary dispute between neighbours. The major cause of the dispute, it
turned out, was grass which had grown across the boundary.

[4]In Mwanda Location where land reform has not yet been implemented because
of technical problems, the people's approach to life is noticeably more
wholesome and relaxed than in other Locations where the reform has been
carried out.

In order to answer this question, I propose in this final section to examine societies where the small-family institution has emerged, matured and become the norm. These societies are, with few exceptions, the developed industrialized countries of Europe and North America. I choose these countries because Kenya is supposedly expected to attain (in the unforeseeable future) a similar economic standard to these societies.

The disappearance of the average large family in industrialized countries is a result but *not* a condition of economic development. But where the non-industrialized countries are concerned, the unquestioned copying of certain 'developed' aspects from industrialized countries as indicators of economic development is reaching the realms of absurdity. One manifestation of this is the belief that a transition from large to small families[5] in the non-industrialized societies is a prerequisite for their economic development (Kirk, 1965). What is unknown to the non-industrialized societies are the social and psychological side-effects of small families and how the industrialized societies are now grappling with the problems generated by the small family.

While the emergence of the small family is a result of industrialization (Muhsam, 1975: 122-140), it is also an indicator of the immense transformation which has occurred in the industrialized societies' populations. This transformation is popularly known as the demographic transition (Kirk, 1965; Cox, 1976: 193-4). The transition, in conjunction with increased life expectancy, sometimes creates a top-heavy population structure, with almost as many old people as young ones. Thus the industrialized societies have what are regarded as 'old' populations compared to the 'young' populations of non-industrialized societies (see Diagram 12.1).

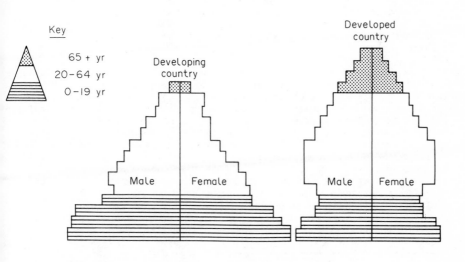

Diagram 12.1.   Population Pyramids of Developing and
                Developed Countries*

*Adapted from Barclay (1966: 224).

---

[5]By 'small', I mean not more than four people - two parents and two children.

140   The Social Cost of Small Families and Land Reform

The shifting of the 'dependence burden' from the bottom to the top of the
population pyramid calls for the allocation of more and more socio-economic
resources as the population of the old keeps on increasing. Illich (1976:
82) indicates what is to come when he says that ". . . 28 percent of the
American budget is spent on the 10 percent of the population who are over
sixty-five. This minority is outgrowing the remainder of the population at
an annual rate of three percent, while the per capita cost of their care is
rising five to seven percent faster than the over-all per capita cost . . .".
As for England,

> ". . . the number of over 85-year-olds (who are by far the most expensive
> to care for) will increase by 50 percent in less than two decades to
> 700,000 people. The strain which some relatives are suffering,
> particularly in an age where there is more tension and frustration could
> prove costly if it leads to mental breakdowns . . . [up to now], there
> has been no serious study of the psychological and social costs of
> caring for the old at home. Certainly some granny-bashing is already
> being registered. . . . If present national trends continue, old people
> will occupy 90 percent of the existing acute female beds by 1991 and
> almost all female psychiatric beds. The shortage of sheltered housing
> has also been well documented: about 20 per cent of the old people
> applying for residential institution in Norfolk merely need a home
> rather than care . . ." (*The Guardian, 1977:* 10).

The problems generated by such an old population will be great and compli-
cated - "an advancing population can stop no more easily than an automobile
rolling down a steep hill" (Sauvy, 1975: 74). A danger therefore exists for
the non-industrialized countries which are striving to produce population
pyramids of the type found in developed countries but without the comparable
economic wealth of the latter; they are also unwittingly in the process of
destroying the traditional social institutions existing in their countries
which support the aged and regard old age with veneration and not as a
problem.[6]

The institution of small nuclear families could be held partially responsible
for the ever-increasing psychological disturbances haunting the industrialized societies. This is because a family which is on average made up of just
two parents (or - increasingly - a one-parent family) and one or two children
offers very limited scope within which a multiplicity of criss-crossing
social interaction can take place. The vertical interaction between parents
(or parent) and children (or child) is confined to the immediate household
environment. So is the horizontal interaction between parents and siblings.
In a family of just two (parent and child), the horizontal interaction
disappears altogether from within the immediate family environment. It is
also absent for the single parent with more than one child; or for the only
child with two parents. In addition, the degree of interaction between
siblings depends very much on their sex and the age separating them, even in
a family of four.

---

[6]Already in 1974/75 Kenya's Ministry of Social Services was giving
financial support to over 200 people in Taita/Taveta District whose age
was on average over 55 years. Abject poverty, having no relatives plus old
age, comprised 64 percent of the recipients' main reasons for being
regarded as distressed cases and thus qualifying for financial help from
the Government. The other reasons were, in rank order: ill-health, deaf/
dumbness, being disabled or mentally retarded, or being an orphan (these are
not, of course, exclusive).

The disappearance of large and/or extended families has led also to the disappearance of large networks of relatives and hence the area within which social interaction can take place is further reduced, and the growing child's experience further limited. This has resulted in both parents and children becoming more dependent on each other's love. Indeed, there is a dearth of human interaction in industrialized societies (Moustakas, 1961; Laing, 1971; Sharpe and Lewis, 1977). For instance, the mother-to-be is left to nurse her pregnancy in isolation. She can, of course, read Dr. Spock and other experts on child-care, and she is usually in contact with her family doctor although these are poor substitutes for the advice and support of female relatives. In such a situation, the support of her husband becomes especially important. In some cases a newlyborn baby sets off a tug-of-war for love between itself and its parents. There is the fear that one of the parents might love the child more than the other spouse. Hence, whoever feels that his/her centrality is threatened, vies for the other's love with the child.

All this creates emotional tension and irritability in the small family household. The battered child and wife syndromes attest to this. In addition, there is the financial side to consider - not only how much a child costs, but also how to keep the family going financially, as well as socially and emotionally. Under these circumstances, it seems two children are the limit for most couples.

In industrialized societies, children are superfluous beings and have become consumer durables.[7] They are not expected to contribute to the material well-being of their families, nor to the day to day maintenance of the household, even if they are able to do so. In contrast, when they become of age they are supposed to fend for themselves and any dependence on parents, or vice versa, is only grudgingly admitted. It is not surprising therefore that the fervour to maintain one's sense of independence and individualism goes as far as sending one's aged parents to be cared for in old people's homes.[8] The type of economic development which has taken place in developed countries has produced the small-family institution and the necessary values and attitudes which justify such self-centred action. Small families in developed countries, situated as they are in a very narrow kin network, insulate children from experiencing the impact of a tragedy such as death. The impact is even further removed with the added advantage of the decline in infant mortality.[9]

---

[7] Indeed, in industrialized societies a whole sub-culture has been built up, orientated towards the child as consumer with his own artificially created 'special requirements' - ranging from Heinz baby foods and Johnson's baby-care products through to nursery rhyme wall-paper and alphabet spaghetti.

[8] Lack of room or the aged's pride of independence are often given as explanations for such action. While they may be partially true, what is forgotten is that these sentiments have become so internalized that they have become part of the cultural milieu. But "for the elderly, the purpose of the home is all too plain - it is somewhere they can be looked after until they die." (Phillips, 1977).

[9] For example, Kenya's Infant Mortality Rate in 1970 was 132 as compared to 22.1, 18.8 and 12.6 for the U.S.A., U.K. and Sweden respectively (Pradervand, 1970).

In Taita, when death occurs, it encompasses people both at the social and personal levels. At the social level, the 'death-quake' affects the whole kin group of the deceased and the community at large. The devastation felt by the individual which the death-quake unleashes depends on how close one is to the deceased. At the personal level, the death-quake affects non-kin members of the community as well as kin. Its impact is mainly personalized in the sense that it induces a delayed socio-psychological reaction on the mourners and causes the individual to reflect on his own life, in isolation of his sorrow. To what intensity and how long this impact will last depends very much on one's age and how often death occurs within one's neighbourhood. In Kenya, one is reminded always of the existence of death because of the practice by Voice of Kenya (VOK) to broadcast 'death-news' daily after the 7 o'clock main news broadcast. It is normal practice for people to be talking while listening to the news, then going completely quiet immediately the announcer says: "Na hizi ndizo habari za vifo" - "And here is the death-news". After this news, people fall back to what they had been doing, passing a cursory remark like "too many people are dying nowadays". But when they hear about the death of a kin or friend, then they usually start to prepare to attend the funeral. Death never ceases to affect people, in spite of (or because of) the daily national publicity it is given. In such a situation, even if the mortality rate is declining (infant and adult) one has a picture of a rising death rate and the natural reaction is to give birth to as many children as possible for fear that some of them may die.[10] Death therefore contributes to the reinforcement of attitudes which favour large families. This is in contrast to the situation in an industrialized country like Great Britain. Only a small minority buy newspaper space in order to announce the death of the 'beloved ones'. These announcements are not always meant to inform distant relatives, but sometimes to serve as notification of a person being dead in case of financial problems arising. While people are saturated with the occurrences of death through the mass media, their presentation is distant and de-personalized and, as such, their impact serves to degrade rather than uphold human life. In the West for most people the death of kin is a rare experience. This is due to the fact that the majority of families rest on a very narrow kin base and, in addition, to the very low infant mortality and the increase in life expectancy resulting from medical care. Hence the occurrence of death is an infrequent event and when it takes place few people are actually affected.

As for those few who are affected by an occurrence of death, on the one hand the sense of loss can be felt intensely because of the lack of a large and close kin group with which to share the sorrow. In some cases the sorrow is so intensely felt that it reaches unhealthy proportions, and can end up by ruining the life of the bereaved. Contributing to this is the fact that the cultural environment demands that sorrow is internalized rather than released.

On the other hand, in the absence of a large kin group the sense of loss is nevertheless minimized by the fact that the majority of the deceased are those who have attained grandparent age. In other words, there is often a considerable generation gap between the deceased and his/her relatives. The death of a grandparent rarely raises any sense of great loss among grand-children because of the lack of alternate generational links.

---

[10]The film *Maragoli* which was produced in Kenya in conjunction with the project from which this book stems, has these sentiments expressed by some of the respondents when they are being interviewed by Dr. Joseph Ssennyonga, the researcher concerned.

Whether the death of a relative is felt intensely or hardly at all, its occurrence, in contrast to Kenya, does not seem to affect one's attitudes towards small families. But even if a large family was desired, one has to contend with the constraints imposed by the economic reality which lead one to having small families rather than large ones.

The limited nature of social interaction and its intensification is particular to small families. The adage 'an Englishman's home is his castle' becomes more relevant, since each family member has his/her own room, indicating that the 'castle' mentality zeroes down to individual rooms within a single house.[11] Children therefore grow up identifying themselves with their rooms, teddy-bears, dolls and toys. It is this private and compartmentalized existence which perhaps led James Hinton to comment, "Our happy Christian homes are the real dark places of the Earth" (Ellis, 1948: 11). Technology in the form of television, the telephone and other luxuries has not been able to solve or compensate for the problems generated by such existence. The socio-psychological claustrophobia immanent in the household environment is at one and the same time both softened and reinforced by the educational system.

The educational system exposes children to a larger community. Through this system, they have social interaction with people who are not members of their families. The success or failure of the individual child to find a friend depends very much on how far parents will 'let go' of him/her. Furthermore, like the toys they own in their bedrooms, children tend to automatically transfer this ownership concept to their human relationships. This is reinforced by the educational system which further instils into them values and attitudes which glorify personal and private attitudes to property.

Right from nursery school the emphasis is on the individual and his/her property. Many books for 3- to 5-year-olds have titles which are aimed at the assertion of the individual. For example: *I Am a Mouse* (Risom, 1969); *Put Me in the Zoo* (Lopshire, 1964); *Are You My Mother?* (Eastman, 1962); *I Know Something You Don't Know* (Agostinelli, 1970); and the *Winnie-The-Pooh* books.[12] One of these, entitled *Reading With Winnie-The-Pooh - Tigger's Book*, has the following rhyme (emphasis in the original):

> I am Tigger, and this is *MY* book.
> I said to Pooh, "I know I am a very bouncy sort of chap,
> but *can't* I have a book of my very own?"
> And Pooh said, "Yes, of course you can, Tigger.
> Even if you *are* a very bouncy sort of Tigger."
> So, this is *MY* book.

The individual is in most cases associated with owning or having a relationship with pets, animals (even fish) and objects, rather than with human beings.

---

[11]This situation is compounded by the residential pattern which is a type of uxorial nomadism, with neighbours having little in common with one another except the socio-economic class the residential area represents.

[12]This sample was taken from the play-school of the University of Sussex.

> "This little fish,"
> I said to Mr. Carp,
> "I want him.
> I like him.
> And he likes me.
> I will call him Otto" (Palmer, 1963).

One might expect that because of the small-family institution, every available chance would be taken to instil into the growing child the importance of its relationship with other members of the family - mother, father, brother and sister. And what better chance of doing this than when teaching 3- to 5-year-olds the alphabet? The following extracts are from a beginners' book (I indicate the obvious omissions in brackets):

(B for Brother):	What begins with B?
	Barber baby bubbles and a bumble bee.
(D for Daddy):	What begins with D?
	David Donald Doo, dreamed a dozen doughnuts and a duck-dog, too.
(F) for Father):	What begins with F?
	Four fluffy feathers on a fiffer-feffer-feff.
(M for Mother or Mummy):	What begins with M?
	Many mumbling mice, are making - a midnight music in the moonlight . . . mighty mice.
(S for Sister):	What begins with S?
	Silly Sammy Slick, sipped six sodas and got sick sick sick (Seuss, 1965).

The type of language actually used in the extracts quoted here is representative of the child's world or sub-culture - which is quite separate from the real (adult) world - on which I have already commented.

The following nursery rhyme comes from a nursery book called *Snuffy* (Bruna, 1970) which is one among many of a similar type which socializes the child towards giving affection to, and to appreciate more, pets, animals and things rather than people:

> Snuffy is a small brown dog,
> with bright black eyes,
> floppy ears,
> and a nice cold nose.

In fact, in some cases, children become so attached to their pets, toys and dolls that they have to be 'weaned' from them (not always successfully - it is not uncommon for a teenager to go to bed clutching his/her old teddybear). However, the weaning does not obliterate the self-centred and possessive attitudes and values which the children have internalized. On the whole, the socialization process of the growing child in industrialized countries is narrow, assertive and individualistic. It is not surprising therefore that even human relationships (especially male/female relationships) become possessively oriented as the phrase 'one-to-one relationship' symbolizes. The growth and belief in romantic monogamistic love is a manifestation of this phenomenon. One wonders how long this belief can last when one considers the weakening of the family institution in the industrialized countries.

The uxorial, mobile and urban pattern of settlement, together with the narrowing down of the kin base and the weakening of the family, has led to the total expunction of certain sexual taboos as far as societies in the industrialized countries are concerned. As an example, it seems that incestuous behaviour is increasingly regarded as such only within the small nuclear family.

It has been noted that generally ". . . sex role and sex behaviour are formed by the joint influence of biology, family and society; to grasp any one period we must know not only its sexual behaviour but its family structure, mores, child-rearing methods, etc." (Karlen, 1971: 4). Responding to the changing culture, sex in industrialized societies has been stripped of its primary function - that of procreation - and at the same time unwrapped from the socio-cultural milieu which provided its mystification. The primary function of sex nowadays is pleasure, supported by a deification of sex as equivalent to love. Hence the equivocation of copulation with the phrase 'making love'.

> ". . . it is to sex that we turn for salvation today. It is our religion, our Golden Land - for many, a purgatory where one waits for failure or bliss, hoping that the time to love has not been, will not be, spent loving badly, the ultimate waste of life . . ." (Karlen, 1971: xix).

In Western industrial societies the relationship between a man and a woman has been torn apart from its familial context; it has become sex-dominated. By dissociating individuals from the respective kin groups they lose the sense of security which stems from the knowledge of being an integral part of a larger social unit. This atomization of society is reflected in increasing numbers of juvenile delinquents, deviants and altogether more and more mentally disturbed people.

Declining fertility in itself cannot insure economic growth. As I have argued in this section, even if the smaller family is associated with overall growing wealth it is not necessarily a good thing all round. In fact it seems that social disorder constitutes the price a society has to pay for the benefits - if there are any real ones - to be derived from Western-style economic development while anomie is likely to be the cost of implementing the small-family norms.

Appendix I

A Sample Registration Form to show how African Labour was Recruited and Controlled

The Chief Registrar of Natives, NAIROBI.	N.A.D Form No. 54/

COMPLAINT OF DESERTION OF REGISTERED NATIVE.

Native's Certificate No.....................Name...................... ....

The above native deserted from my employ ....
.......(date)

He was engaged on........................... .on.................days verbal contract
.........(date)   ....months written contract

at...
....(place)   ((will attend or to produce evidence
I wish to prosecute him for this offence and hereby agree to appear to give evidence
if and when called upon
....
Signature of Employer.

Address ....
....

Date.......................................

The Chief Registrar of Natives, NAIROBI.	N.A.D Form No. 54/ ....

COMPLAINT OF DESERTION OF REGISTERED NATIVE.

Native's Certificate No..........................Name...

The above native deserted from my employ...
......(date)

He was engaged on...on.....................days verbal contract
....(date)   ....months written contract

at...
....(place)   (will attend or to produce evidence
I wish to prosecute him for this offence and hereby agree to appear to give evidence
if and when called upon.
....
Signature of Employer

Address ....
....

Date...

The Chief Registrar of Natives, NAIROBI.	N.A.D. Form No 54/.... .

COMPLAINT OF DESERTION OF REGISTERED NATIVE.

Native's Certificate No...........................Name.. .

The above native deserted from my employ..
......(date)

He was engaged on...........................on....................days verbal contract
....(date)   ....months written contract

at...
....(place)   (will attend or to produce evidence
I wish to prosecute him for this offence and hereby agree to appear to give evidence
it and when called upon.
....
Signature of Employer.

Address ....

Date...

Reprinted with kind permission from W. McGregor Ross
Kenya from within: A short political history,
Allen & Unwin, p. 196.

Appendix II

Terms of Reference for the Kenya Land Commission appointed April 1932

(1) To consider the needs of the native population, present and prospective, with respect to land, whether to be held on tribal or individual tenure.

(2) To consider the desirability and practibility of setting aside further areas of land for the present and future occupancy of -
(a) communities, bodies or individual natives of recognized tribes; and
(b) detribalized natives, that is, natives who belong to no tribe or who have severed connexion with the tribe to which they once belonged.

(3) To determine the nature and extent of claims asserted by natives over land alienated to non-natives and to make recommendations for the adequate settlement of such claims whether by legislation or otherwise.

(4) To examine claims asserted by natives over land not yet alienated and to make recommendations for the adequate settlement of such claims.

(5) To consider the nature and extent of the rights held by natives under Section 86 of the Crown Lands Ordinance, and whether better means could be adopted for dealing with such rights in respect of -
(a) land already alienated; and
(b) land alienated in the future.

(6) To define the area generally known as the Highlands within which persons of European descent are to have a privileged position in accordance with the White Paper 1923.

(7) To review the working of the Native Lands Trust Ordinance, 1930, and to consider how any administrative difficulties that already may have arisen can best be met whether by supplemented legislation or otherwise without involving any departure from the principles of the said Ordinance.

Source: KLC, 1933: 1-2.

Appendix III

Population Pyramids of Shigaro-Sungululu and
the Household Sample

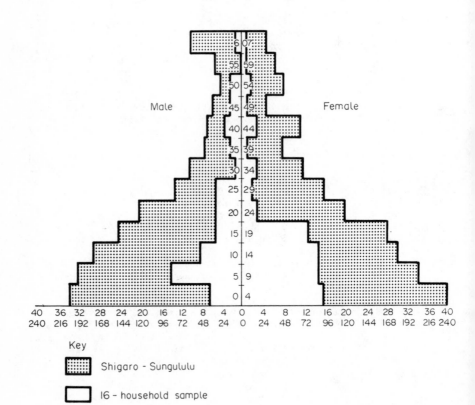

Key

Shigaro - Sungululu

16 - household sample

Appendix IV

Major Activities of Sample Households Listed in Order of
Frequency done by Stratum

Frequency ranking order	Whole sample	Strata			
		One	Two	Three	Four
1	Cooking	Cooking	Cooking	Cooking	School
2	Water-fetching	Cash labour	Water-fetching	Herding	*Shamba* work
3	*Shamba* work	*Shamba* work	*Shamba* work	Water-fetching	Cash labour
4	School	Housework	Visits and journeys	School	Water-fetching
5	Herding	Visits and journeys	Milking	*Shamba* work	Leisure
6	Leisure	Social labour	Herding	Leisure	Cooking
7	Housework	Water-fetching	Leisure	Housework	Firewood-collecting
8	Firewood-collecting	Leisure	Housework	Firewood-collecting	Errands and shopping
9	Visits and journeys	Firewood-collecting	School	Errands and shopping	Social labour
10	Cash labour	Herding	Firewood-collecting	Visits and journeys	Child-minding
11	Milking	Child-minding	Illness	Others	Visits and journeys
12	Errands and shopping	School	Social labour	Child-minding	Herding
13	Social labour	Others	Errands and shopping	Social labour	Housework
14	Others	Illness	Cash labour	Cash labour	Others
15	Illness	Errands and shopping	Others	Illness	Illness
16	Child-minding	–	Child-minding	Milking	–

Appendix V

Survey of Kenya: Shigaro-Sungululu Registration Section Map[+]

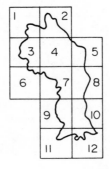

[+]The boundaries on this map are not necessarily strictly accurate.

Appendix VI

Agricultural Statistics of Wundanyi Estate

Year	1923	1924	1925	1926
Total acres cultivated	190	190	173	188
Acres under coffee cultivation	173	173	173	188
Exported coffee in tons	5.50	18.00	19.35	20.00
Wataita employed	50	70	82	–

Source: Nazzaro, 1974: 97, Table 3.

Bibliography

Unpublished Materials

Epstein, T. S., "Research Proposal: A Cross-cultural Study of the Impact of
    Population Growth on the Distribution of Income in Rural Communities",
    Institute of Development Studies (IDS) at the University of Sussex, 1973.
Harris, A. H. and G. C., "Interim Report to the Colonial Social Science
    Research Council", December 1952.
Mashengu wa Mwachofi, "Land Consolidation in Mwanda Location: Agents of
    Change and Relationship to the Community", Dept. of Sociology, University
    of Nairobi, B.A. Dissertation Paper, August/September 1975.
Mwachala, H. A., "'Mlagui Mganga': The Witch-Doctor, the Goat and the
    Intestines", Mwasungia, Wundanyi, April 7, 1972.
Mwang'ombe, Archbishop, "Mizango Ya Kidawida" (Kidawida Traditions and
    Practices), Mombasa, 1952; translated by Shete, H. M., Mgange-Nyika,
    Taita, 1976.

Government Publications and Documents

(1) Government of Colony and Protectorate of Kenya

African Affairs Department, *Annual Report* 1931-1960, Government Printer,
    Nairobi, 1960.
Humphrey, N., *The Kikuyu Lands*, Govt. Printer, Nairobi, 1945.
Humphrey, N., *Sociological Aspects of Some Agricultural Problems of North
    Kavirondo: The Liguru and the Land*, Govt. Printer, Nairobi, 1947.
Kenya Land Commission Evidence, Vol. 3, Govt. Printer, Nairobi, 1934.
Kenya Land Commission Report, Govt. Printer, Nairobi, 1933.
Kenya Population Census, 1962.
Ministry of Agriculture, Animal Husbandry and Water Resources, *African Land
    Development in Kenya 1946-62*, 1962.
Report on Native Affairs 1939-45, Govt. Printer, Nairobi, 1947.
Sessional Paper No. 2 of 1958/59.
Statistical Abstract, Nairobi, 1975.
Survey of Kenya, Nairobi, 1970.
Swynnerton, R. J. M., *A Plan to Intensify the Development of African
    Agriculture in Kenya*, Govt. Printer, Nairobi, 1954.

(2) Republic of Kenya

African Socialism and its Application to Planning in Kenya, Govt. Printer,
     Nairobi, 1965.
Development Plan 1970/74.
Development Plan 1974/78.
File No. EPD/SC 2/059, 16 March 1977.
Integrated Rural Survey 1974-75: Basic Report, Central Bureau of Statistics,
     Ministry of Finance, March 1977.
Kenya Gazette Supplement Bills 1967, "The Vagrancy Bill", 1967, Govt.
     Printer, Nairobi, 24 January 1967.
Kenya Population Census 1969, Statistics Division, Ministry of Finance and
     Economic Planning.
The *National Assembly Official Report*, Vol. XXIX, 1973.
Taita/Taveta District, *Annual Report 1976*, District Commissioner
     Wundanyi.
*Urban Population Projections During 1969-2000 Within the Context of Urban
     Development Strategy*, Ministry of Finance and Planning, 1974.

Newspapers and Periodicals

The Guardian, "Old age is the coming thing", London/Manchester, 8 August 1977.
Journal of African Administration (JAA), Special Supplement, The Arusha
     Conference Report on African Land Tenure in East and Central Africa, 1956.
The Listener, "Wiping out Kenya's elephants: who's to blame?", BBC
     Publications, London, 9 June 1977.
New Internationalist, Blackfriars Press, Leicester, June 1977.

Books and Journals

Agostinelli, E. (1970) *I Know Something You Don't Know*, Ernest Benn Ltd.,
     London.
Baran, P. A. (1957) *The Political Economy of Growth*, Monthly Review Press,
     New York.
Baran, P. A. and Sweezy, P. M. (1966) *Monopoly Capital*, Monthly Review Press,
     New York.
Barclay, G. W. (1966) *Techniques and Population Analysis*, Wiley.
Barnett, D. L. and Karari Njama (1966) *Mau Mau From Within: an autobiography
     and analysis of Kenya's Peasant Revolt*, MacGibbon and Kee, London.
Beck, A. (1970) *A History of the British Medical Administration of East
     Africa 1900-1950*, Harvard University Press.
Behrman, S. J. (*et al.*) (1969) *Fertility and Family Planning: A World View*,
     University of Michigan Press.
Berelson (*et al.*) (1969) *Family Planning and Population Programs*, University
     of Chicago Press, 4th Impression.
Berg-Schlosser, D. (1970) "The distribution of income and education in Kenya:
     Causes and potential political consequences", *Weltforum*, Verlag, Munich.
Bernstein, H. (1971) "Modernization Theory and the Sociological Study of
     Development", in *The Journal of Development Studies*, Vol. 7, January,
     No. 2, Frank Cass & Co. Ltd., London.
Berry, E. (1977) "David's Obligation", *New Society*, New Science Publications,
     London, 8 Sept.
Bigsten, A. (1976) *Regional Inequality and Development in Kenya*, University
     of Gothenburg, Sweden.
Boeke, J. H. (1968) *Economics and Economic Policy of Dual Societies as
     Exemplified by Indonesia*, University Microfilms, Ann Arbor.

Bondestam, L. (1978) *Population Growth in Kenya*, Research Report No. 12, Scandinavian Institute of African Studies.

Bostock, Rev. P. G. (1950) *The Peoples of Kenya: The Taita*, Macmillan, London.

Brett, E. A. (1973) *Colonialism and Underdevelopment in East Africa*, Heinemann, London.

Bruna, D. (1970) *Snuffy*, Methuen & Co. Ltd., London.

Clayton, E. S. (1959) "Policies Affecting Agrarian Development in Kenya", in the *East African Economics Review*, Vol. 5, No. 2, January.

Cliffe, L. (1973) *Rural Class Formation in East Africa*, Discussion Paper, Centre of International and Area Studies, University of London.

Cohn, N. (1957) *The Pursuit of the Millenium*, Secker and Warburg.

Court, D. and Ghai, D. (eds.) (1974) *Education, Society and Development – New Perspectives from Kenya*, OUP, Nairobi.

Cox, P. R. (1976) *Demography*, 5th Edition, Cambridge University Press.

Dore, R. (1976) *The Diploma Disease: Education, Qualification and Development*, George Allen & Unwin Ltd., London.

Dorner, P. (1972) *Land Reform and Economic Development*, Penguin Books.

Dumont, R. (1957) *Types of Rural Economy*, Methuen, London.

Eastman, P. D. (1962) *Are You My Mother?*, Collins-Clear-Type Press, London.

Ehrlich, P. R. (1971) *The Population Bomb*, Pan Books Ltd.

Ellis, H. (1936) *Studies in the Psychology of Sex*, Vol. IV, Random House, New York.

Ellis, H. (1948) *On Life and Sex*, Heinemann.

Epstein, T. S. (1973) *South India: Yesterday, Today and Tomorrow – Mysore villages revisited*, Macmillan, London.

Epstein, T. S. and Jackson, D. (eds.) (1975) *The Paradox of Poverty*, Macmillan, New Delhi.

Fisher, J. L. and Potter, N. (1969) "Natural Resource Adequacy for the United States and the World", in Philip M. Hauser (ed.), *The Population Dilemma*, 2nd Edition, Prentice-Hall, Inc., Englewood Cliffs, New Jersey.

Frank, A. G. (1969) *Capitalism and Underdevelopment in Latin America: Historical Studies of Chile and Brazil*, Monthly Review Press, New York and London.

Furtado, C. (1977) "Development", in *International Social Science Journal*, Vol. XXIX, No. 4.

George, S. (1976) *How the Other Half Dies: The Real Reasons for World Hunger*, Penguin Books.

Gersovitz, M. (1975) *Land Reform: Some Theoretical Considerations*, Department of Economics Research Report No. 7518, University of Western Ontario.

Glasser, B. G. and Strauss, A. C. (1977) *The Discovery of the Grounded Theory: Strategies for qualitative research*, 8th Printing, Aldine Publishing Co., Chicago.

Gluckman, M. (1962) "Kinship and Marriage among the Lozi of Northern Rhodesia and the Zulu of Natal", in A.R. Radcliffe-Brown and D. Forde (eds.), *African Systems of Kinship and Marriage*, OUP, London, Reprint.

Godfrey, E. M. (1973) *Technical and Vocational Training in Kenya and Harambee Institutes of Technology*, Discussion Paper No. 169, Institute of Development Studies, University of Nairobi, June.

Godfrey, M. and Langdon, S. (1976) "Partners in Underdevelopment? The Transnationalization Thesis in a Kenyan Context", in *The Journal of Commonwealth and Comparative Politics*, Vol. XIV, No. 1, Frank Cass & Co. Ltd., London.

Godfrey, M. and Mutiso, G. C. M. (1974) "The Political Economy of Self-help: Kenya's Harambee Institutes of Technology", in *The Canadian Journal of African Studies*.

Goldschmidt, W. (1976) Culture and Behaviour of the Sebei: *A Study in Continuity and Adaptation*, University of California Press.

Gould, J. and Kolb, W. L. (eds.) (1964) *A Dictionary of the Social Services*,
    Tavistock Publications.
Gray and Gulliver (eds.) (1964) *The Family Estate in Africa*, Routledge &
    Kegan Paul, London.
Gray, R. and Birmingham, D. (eds.) (1970) *Pre-Colonial Africa Trade*, OUP,
    London.
Hauser, P. M. (ed.) (1969) *The Population Dilemma*, 2nd Edition, Prentice-
    Hall Inc., Englewood Cliffs, New Jersey.
Heyer, J., Maitha, J. K. and Senga, W. M. (eds.) (1976) *Agricultural
    Development in Kenya: An Economic Assessment*, OUP, Nairobi.
Holtham, G. and Hazelwood, A. (1976) *Aid and Inequality in Kenya*, Overseas
    Development Institute, London.
Huxley, E. (1953) *White Man's Country*, Vols. I and II, Chatto & Windus,
    London (new Edition).
IBRD (1974) *Land Reform*, World Bank Paper, Rural Development Series.
IBRD and IDA (1973) Report No. 2549-KE. Agricultural Sector Survey - Kenya,
    Vol. 1, 20 December.
Iliffe, J. (1969) *Tanganyika Under German Rule 1905-1912*, Cambridge
    University Press.
Illich, I. (1976) *Limits to Medicine, Medical Nemesis: The Expropriation of
    Health*, Open Forum, A. Marion Boyars Book, London.
IPPF (1964) *Sex and Human Relations*, Proceedings of Fourth Conference
    (London 8-11 June, 1964), Excerpta Medica Foundation, Amsterdam.
Itote, W. (General China) (1967) *'Mau Mau' General*, East African Publishing
    House.
Jolly, R. (ed.) (1978) *Disarmament and World Development*, Pergamon Press,
    Oxford.
Kariuki, J. M. (1963) *Mau Mau Detainee*, OUP, London.
Karlen, Arno (1971) *Sexuality and Homosexuality*, Macdonald, London.
Kenyatta, J. (1961) *Facing Mount Kenya*, Mercury Books.
Kimambo, I. (1970) "The Economic History of the Kamba 1850-1950", in
    B. A. Ogot (ed.), *Hadith 2*, East African Publishing House, Nairobi.
Kirk, D. (1965) "Natality in the Developing Countries: Recent Trends and
    Prospects", in Behrman *et al.* (eds.), *Fertility and Family Planning*,
    University of Michigan Press.
Kjekshus, H. (1977) *Ecology Control and Economic Development in East
    African History: The Case of Tanganyika, 1850-1950*, Heinemann, London.
Koestenbaum, P. (1974) *Existential Sexuality: Choosing to Love*, Prentice-Hall
    Inc., Englewood Cliffs, New Jersey.
Kuczynski, R. R. (1949) *Demographic Survey of the British Colonial Empire*,
    Vol. II, OUP.
Laing, R. D. (1971) *The Politics of the Family and Other Essays*, Tavistock
    Publications, London.
Lamb, G. (1974) Peasant Politics: *Conflict and Development in Murang'a*,
    Julien Friedmann Publishers Ltd., Lewes.
Leys, C. (1975) Underdevelopment in Kenya: *The Political Economy of Neo-
    Colonialism 1964-1971*, Heinemann, London.
Leys, N. (1924) *Kenya*, Leonard & Virginia Woolfe, London.
Lipton, M. (1975) "Towards a Theory of Land Reform", in D. Lehmann (ed.),
    Agricultural Reform and Agricultural Reformism, Faber, London.
Liszka, S. W., Jr. (1974) "A Preliminary Report on Research on the Origins
    and Internal Migrations of the Taita People", in *Mila* - a biannual
    newsletter of cultural research, Vol. IV, No. 2, Institute of African
    Studies, University of Nairobi.
Long, N. (1977) *An Introduction to the Sociology of Rural Development*,
    Tavistock Publications, London.
Lopshire, R. (1964) *Put Me in the Zoo*, Collins & Harvill, London.
Madoka, Rev. A. (1950) *Taita na Kanisa La Kristo: Katika Miaka Hamsini,
    1900-1950*, Taita Rural Deanery, Wusi, Kenya.

Marx, K. (1977) *Capital* (vols. I-III), Lawrence & Wishart, London, Reprint.

McClelland, D. (1961) *The Achieving Society*, Free Press, New York.

Meier, G. M. (1964) *Leading Issues in Development Economics: Selected Materials and Commentary*, OUP, New York.

Meier, R. L. (1965) *Developmental Planning*, McGraw-Hill.

Middleton, J. (ed.) (1967) *Magic, Witchcraft and Curing*, The Natural History Press, New York.

Milne, A. A. (1966) *Reading with Winnie-The-Pooh: Tigger's Book*, Nelson.

Mkangi, G. C. (1975) "Land Tenure, Population Growth and Economic Differentiation: The Ribe Tribe of Kenya", in T. S. Epstein and D. Jackson (eds.), *The Paradox of Poverty: Socio-economic Aspects of Population Growth*, MacMillan of India.

Mkangi, G. C. (1977) "Education, Poverty and Fertility among the Wataita of Kenya", in T. S. Epstein and D. Jackson (eds.), *The Feasibility of Fertility Planning*, Pergamon Press, Oxford & New York.

Moorman, J. and Ingram, M. (1975) *The Population Problem: A challenge to the people of our time*, Search Press Ltd., London.

Moustakas, E. C. (1961) *Loneliness*, A Spectrum Book, Prentice-Hall Inc.

Muhsam, H. V. (1975) *Education and Population: mutual impacts*, International Union for the Scientific Study of Population (IUSSP).

Mukwaya, A. B.   *Land Tenure in Buganda*, East African Studies, No. 1.

Murray-Brown, J. (1972) *Kenyatta*, George Allen & Unwin, London.

Myrdal, G. (1971) *The Challenge of World Poverty - A World Anti-Poverty Programme in Outline*, Pelican Books, London.

Nag, M. *et al.* (1977) "Economic Value of Children in Two Peasant Societies", in *International Population Conference*, Mexico.

Nazzaro, A. A. (1974) *Changing Use of the Resource Base Among the Taita of Kenya*, Ph.D. Thesis submitted to Michigan State University, Xerox University Microfilms, Michigan State University.

New, C. (1971) *Life Wanderings and Labours in Eastern Africa*, 3rd Edition, Frank Cass, London.

Odinga, O. (1967) *Not Yet Uhuru*, Heinemann, London.

Ogot, B. A. and Kieran, J. A. (eds.) (1968) *Zamani: A Survey of East African History*, East Africa Publishing House, Nairobi.

O'Keefe, P. (1975) *Gakarara - A Study in Development of Underdevelopment*, Occasional Paper No. 6, Disaster Research Unit, University of Bradford.

Okoth-Ogendo, H. W. O. (1976) "African Land Tenure Reform" in J. Heyer, J. K. Maitha and W. M. Senga (eds.), *Agricultural Development in Kenya: An Economic Assessment*, OUP, Nairobi.

Palmer, H. (1963) *A Fish Out of Water*, Collins Clear-Type Press, London.

Parkin, D. J. (1972) *Palms, Wine and Witnesses: Public Spirit and Private Gain in an African Farming Community*, Intertext Books, London.

Parkin, D. J. (1969) *Neighbours and Nationals in an African City Ward*, Routledge.

Parsons, T. (1964) "Evolutionary Universals in Society", in *American Sociological Review*, Vol. 29, No. 3.

Parsons, T. (1966) *Society's Evolutionary Perspectives*, Englewood Cliffs, New Jersey.

Parsons, T. (1968) *The Structure of Social Action* (2 vols.), New York.

Peel, J. and Carr, G. (1975) *Contraception and Family Design*, Churchill Livingstone, Edinburgh.

Peet, R. C. and White, B. (1977) "Economic Value of Children in Two Peasant Societies", in *International Population Conference*, Vol. I, Mexico.

Phillips, M. (1977) "Home for the Old", *New Society*, New Science Publications, London, 7 March.

Pradervand, P. (1970) *Family Planning Programmes in Africa*, Development Centre of the Organization for Economic Co-operation and Development, Paris.

Quiggin, A. H. (1949) *Trade Routes, Trade and Currency in East Africa,*
    Occasional Papers of the Rhodes-Livingstone Museum, Livingstone.
Ranger, T. O. (ed.) (1968) *Aspects of Central African History,* Heinemann,
    London.
Risom, O. (1966) *I Am A Mouse,* Paul Hamlyn, London.
Rodney, W. (1972) *How Europe Underdeveloped Africa,* Bagle-L'Ouverture,
    London & Tanzania Publishing House, Dar-es-Salaam.
Ross, W. McGregor (1927) *Kenya From Within: A Short Political History,*
    George Allen & Unwin, London.
Rostow, W. W. (1967) *The Stages of Economic Growth; A Non-Communist
    Manifesto,* Cambridge.
Sauvy, A. (1975) *Zero Growth?* A. Maguire, trans., Blackwell, Oxford.
Seers, D. (1972) *What are we trying to measure?,* IDS Reprints No. 106,
    University of Sussex, April.
Seers, D. (1979) "Patterns of Dependence", in José J. Villamil (ed.)
    Transnational Capitalism and National Development, Harvester, Hassocks.
Segal, A. (1972) "The Politics of Land in East Africa", in N.T. Uphoff and
    W. F. Ilchman (eds.), *The Political Economy of Development - Theoretical
    and Empirical Contributions,* University of California Press.
Seuss, Dr. (1965) *Dr. Seuss's ABC,* Beginner Books, Collins & Harvill.
Shanin, T. (ed.) (1971) *Peasants and Peasant Societies: Selected Readings,*
    Penguin Books.
Sharpe, R. and Lewis, D. (1977) *Thrive on Stress,* Souvenir Press, London.
Simmons, A. B. (1977) "The Value of Children (VOC) approach in population
    policies: new hope or false promise?", in *International Population
    Conference,* Vol. I, Mexico.
Soja, E. W. (1968) *The Geography of Modernization in Kenya: A special
    analysis of social, economic and political change,* Syracuse University
    Press.
Somerset, A. (1977) "Aptitude Tests, Socio-Economic Background and Secondary
    School Selection: The Possibilities and Limits of Change", a Paper
    Presented at *Bellagio Conference on Social Science Research and
    Educational Effectiveness,* August.
Somjee, S. H. (1980) *Kipande: the Symbol of Imperialism (1915-1948): A Study
    in Colonial Material Culture,* Staff Seminar Paper, Department of
    Literature, University of Nairobi.
Sorrenson, M. P. K. (1968) *Origins of European Settlement in Kenya,* OUP,
    Nairobi.
Spear, T. T. (1974) "Traditional Myths and Historians' Myths: Variations on
    the Singwaya Theme of Mijikenda Origins", in *History in Africa,* 1.
Spear, T. T. (1977) "Traditional Myths and Linguistic Analysis: Singwaya
    Revisited", in *History in Africa,* 4.
Sunkel, O. (1976) *The Development of Development Thinking,* Keynote Address,
    at the 1st Inter-Regional Meeting on Development Research, Communication
    and Education, IDS, University of Sussex, September.
Temu (1972) "The Giriama War, 1914-15" in B. Ogot (ed.), *War and Society in
    East Africa,* Frank Cass, London.
Thuku, H. (1970) *Harry Thuku - An Autobiography,* OUP.
U.N. Department of Economic and Social Affairs (1976) *Progress in Land
    Reform,* 6th Report, Sales No. 76, IV.
Van Zwanenberg, R. M. A. and King, A. (1975) *An Economic History of Kenya
    and Uganda 1800-1970,* MacMillan, London.
Verhelst, T. (1968) *Materials on Land Law and Economic Development in Africa,*
    School of Law and the African Studies Centre, University of California,
    unpublished Preliminary Edition.
Wassermen, G. (1973) "Continuity and Counter-Insurgency: The Role of Land
    Reform in Decolonizing Kenya - 1962-70", in *The Canadian Journal of
    African Studies,* Vol. VII, No. 1.

Weber, M. (1963) *The Sociology of Religion*, E. Fishoff, trans., Beacon Press, Mass.

Weinrich, A. K. H. (1975) "African Farmers in Rhodesia: Old and New Peasant Communities in Karangaland", in *International African Institute* (IAI).

Winter, E. H.   *Bwamba Economy*, East African Studies, No. 5.

Wisner, B. (1976) *Man-made Famine in Eastern Kenya: The Interrelationships of Environment and Development*, IDS Discussion Paper, No. 96, University of Sussex, July.

Wolff, R. D. (1974) *The Economics of Colonialism – Britain and Kenya, 1870–1930*, Yale University Press.

World Bank (1976) *Atlas: Population, Per Capita Product and Growth Rates*, World Bank.

Yinger, J. M. (1961) *Religion in the Struggle for Power: A Study in the Sociology of Religion*, Russell & Russell, Inc., New York.

Yoshida, M. (1971) "The Protected Development of Kenya", in *Journal of Rural Development*.

Index